→30

HEAD OVER HEELS

Joanne Woodward & Paul Newman

HEAD OVER HEELS

A Love Affair in Words and Pictures

MELISSA NEWMAN

Edited by Andrew Kelly

VORACIOUS

Little, Brown and Company

New York Boston London

Including photographs by

Richard Avedon
Sid Avery
Ralph Crane
Bruce Davidson
John Engstead
Leo Fuchs
A. Louis Goldman
Milton H. Greene
Philippe Halsman
John R. Hamilton
Gene Lesser
Roger Marshutz
Leonard McCombe
Gordon Parks
George Rinhart
Sanford Roth
Roy Schatt
Lawrence Schiller
Sam Shaw
Bradley Smith
Stewart Stern
Ulrich Strauss
David Sutton
Philippe Le Tellier

"I shall lock myself in an abandoned water closet I love you so very much. And shut my mouth and carry on in silent communion with your soul." —*Paul Newman*

They were beautiful.

They were movie stars.

They were also my parents. The photographs don't lie.

I grew up surrounded by extraordinary pictures. They tether me to a layered history, a strange world where the people who read me storybooks and went sledding and cooked breakfast existed also as chameleons, shiny objects in an alternate universe.

My Connecticut childhood unfolds in shades of black and white and in the muted palette of 1960s 8mm film. We would gather on the couch, sifting through snapshots, or listening to the stutter of the projector, watching home movies on a rickety pull-down screen. The memories that remain with me are memories of *images*.

°°°°

For a time, my husband and I lived together in a very old saltbox where the only two pictures of family were one of my father riding hell-bent for leather toward the camera on a wild-eyed horse, and one of my mother wearing nothing but fishnet stockings, pasties, and white balloons. If anyone asked, I would say, with all the honesty of omission, that my dad was a cowboy. And my mom was a stripper.

°°°°

My sister Nell, Beverly Hills, 1960 (Paul Newman)

He knew how to wield a hammer, my father, especially when it came to hanging pictures. Lips clamped shut around several tiny nails, he would scan the wall looking for an empty spot. There have always been wall-fulls of images in the family house where we now live, an evolving gallery, meticulously jammed together like pieces of a jigsaw puzzle.

Predictable pets and birthday babies give way to some distinctive outliers. A cowboy pops a wheelie on a motorcycle. A lithe woman in an evening gown poses ankle deep in the ocean, a man hangs upside down next to a giant sailfish. Duke Ellington and Louis Armstrong plug their ears as my father, between them, attempts to play the trombone. My mother, in a home-made dress, clutches her Academy Award. In countless other framed incarnations—blonde, redhead, brunette—she is repeatedly unrecognizable.

As a child, such images were normal to me. Contrived glamour shots, movie stills with strange costumes and stranger situations—these were pictures of my parents. I never thought to ask why.

° ° ° °

The photographs are not static for me; they are more of a constant, a throughline. Although they observe an ever-evolving *me* with their fixed eyes, we have grown up together, blessed and burdened by changing contexts.

It is impossible for casual visitors to make it through the house without being distracted for a century or two on their way to the living room. We locate them eventually, wedged in a corner, gazing at the frames on the wall, transfixed. "Who *are* these people?" they say.

° ° ° °

We are standing in the kitchen. "I have never washed a dog in this sink in my life!" my mother says with a rising southern twang. She is indignant.

She is also in denial. Just around the corner hangs a black and white picture of Joanne Woodward, movie star, hair permed in '80s glory. Sleeves rolled, she is soaping up a terrier in the very sink before which we now stand. It's such a sweetly satisfying thought. I say nothing.

° ° ° °

We love this creaky old place, its nineteenth-century hardware, its persistent evolution toward decrepitude. We love the things that get fixed and then immediately unravel. We like to call them "features." Sylvester Stallone, after attending a meeting here with my father, was rumored to have remarked to one of his assistants on the way home, "Who would ever think Paul Newman

Westport, Connecticut, 1988 (Paul Newman)

would live in a shitbox like that?" He is welcome to contest this, but we consider it a point of pride, and may someday have it chiseled over the front door.

At least the cracked plaster is invisible, hidden behind layers of photographs. My parents bought the house in 1961, the year I was born, and my husband and I bought it from them forty years later. They had not bothered to inspect the termite-riddled floors, or anything else really. Pots and pans always dotted the carpet during rainstorms. They were untroubled by the mundanities of home maintenance. They were *actors*. And they were in love.

° ° ° °

There are certain pictures of my parents in their favorite trysting spots—floating on the river behind the house in an inflatable raft or perched on the precarious stairs of the tree house. These have always remained in view, mixed in with children in tutus and swaddled babies, perhaps a reminder that escape is always possible, and one doesn't have to go very far.

° ° ° °

Beverly Hills, 1967 (Joanne Woodward)

The doors to their bedroom, with comically large bolts, functioned like an air lock. When I was quite small, I wondered why a room would need *two* doors, as I blithely flung myself between my parents in their warm bed. There was a door knocker but I could hardly reach it, much less see that it was two cherubs kissing. I loved the musky smell of that unmade bed. No doubt I almost witnessed the ultimate intimacy firsthand, long before I would have known what to call it.

 ° ° ° °

Of course, I never knew it was by Lawrence Schiller, the photo. It hung unobtrusively in the back stairwell—a small, hidden shrine to the mystery of romance. In it my father gently lifts my mother's skirt with a finger, while she coyly holds it down, laughing. He stares at the camera with a slightly goofy but proprietary grin. This is what I think of when I think of their relationship. The Schiller photo. The look on his face, the feigned bashfulness on her part.

 ° ° ° °

Both of my parents (and many of their friends) took beautiful pictures. But, unsurprisingly, they...*we*...were chronicled by a veritable *Who's Who* of photographers, a fact that became evident as I gathered together images for this project, which proved to be very different from the one I had daydreamed about forever. What I imagined being a simple process of emptying skinny wooden frames into a book and presenting it to the world became, instead, a deep dive into provenance and attribution.

It has been an unexpectedly moving journey. People have stories. It seems that the experience of creating these pictures left its mark on their makers, something I deeply understand. I can be alone in a room, poring over stacks of weighty matte photo paper with unreadable inscriptions and curled edges, and still feel a sharp intake of breath at the achingly beautiful movie stars who happen to be my parents.

◦◦◦◦

I skitter downstairs at two in the morning, flip open the laptop, and click "Buy." The internet is a black hole, especially when you know you might find, at any moment, pristine contact sheets by Philippe Halsman…taken in your living room. My parents, in a series of several images, sharing a cigarette. It's the sixties. It's very funny. I justify the expense by telling myself it's not a purchase, it's a repatriation.

◦◦◦◦

Along with my parents' house, I inherited the curse of nostalgia. In every closet are bags and boxes, layers of ephemera stretching back to the Cretaceous era. Theirs, mine, a sea of words and images.

Sifting through report cards, moth wings, and middle-school valentines, I grab a random handful of paper. Artifacts seem to sprout like mushrooms, even in this picked-over attic. Nothing can be tossed without being carefully examined. I am an archaeologist. I uncurl my fingers. In my hand are what appear to be the first ten letters my father wrote my mother. Ever.

Over time, my blushing embarrassment has reached a detente with detachment around these things, but still I am struck by a complex set of emotions. I contemplate not opening them.

They are juicy and passionate. Sophomoric. It's obvious he fell fast, and I imagine her as he describes her—the seductress, the free spirit that would lead him from his bourgeois upbringing to the bohemian he longed to be. My mother was the more inevitable artist, a woman so instinctively herself even her genteel southern roots couldn't compromise her. He was a man uncertain of who he was. It's easy to understand why he was smitten.

The next week of sifting yields a large stack of telegrams sent to my mother after she won the Oscar in 1957. On top is one from Ingrid Bergman. Tucked in the middle is a blue envelope containing a vaguely snarky congratulation from Joan Crawford: "I have heard such wonderful reports of your great willingness to learn."

◦◦◦◦

In the breakfast room is a photo of my mother, clear eyed, unadorned, androgynous. She has been caught, lips slightly parted, as though she is about to speak. She's just cut all her hair off with fingernail scissors. It's a defiant response to the studio's attempt to give her gun-toting tomboy character a teased 1950s coif. The studio is furious. My mother looks extraordinary.

····

My parents always kept an eye out for opportunities to collaborate. Some of that work is forgettable, some remarkable. My father loved to direct my mother, and he nurtured some of her deepest and most complex performances. She was his favorite actress, and she knew it. A photograph from the set of *Rachel, Rachel* shows my father hovering protectively over my mother, who lies on the ground, being embraced by another man. I have scrutinized his face, trying to discern what he is thinking. As a director, he had repeatedly balked at shooting this scene, arguing it was unnecessary or could be accomplished less directly or somehow obscured. He is, I like to think, jealous.

····

They taught me about passion, and, more importantly, they taught me about long-lived passion, the kind that spills over into art and life, that makes sharing coffee at the breakfast table an act as affirming as the carnal act that may or may not have preceded it.

My father carried a small, folded leather picture frame in his suitcase. No doubt my mother gave it to him to remind him of what would be waiting when he got home if he played his cards right. Inside is a double image of the two of them, two variations of the moment just before a kiss.

····

My parents were inexorable, they were *forever*. They chose each other over and over, sometimes in spite of, sometimes because of. It wasn't always a fairy tale, but I wanted to remember the best, dreamiest, most sublime part, and that part just happens to be true.

This book is my gift to them, to myself, and to you.

Downstairs bedroom door, Westport, Connecticut, 2023 (Jerri Graham)

16   Saugatuck River, Westport, Connecticut, 1965 (Bruce Davidson)

El Rancho Hotel, Las Vegas, 1958 (Stewart Stern)

Westport, Connecticut, 2023 (Jerri Graham)

El Rancho Hotel, Las Vegas, 1958 (Stewart Stern)

New York, 1955 (Joanne Woodward)

Westport, Connecticut, 2023 (Jerri Graham)

On break while filming *The Long, Hot Summer*, Jackson, Louisiana, 1958

"I was auditioning on a hot August day, sitting out talking to a friend of mine who was the agency's receptionist, and then walked in what looked like an advertisement for an ice cream soda, and there was Paul, in a seersucker suit looking so pristine no sweat big blue eyes lots of curly brown hair, and I thought 'Oh, that's disgusting.'" —*Joanne Woodward*

With Sanford Roth's cat at Griffith Park Zoo, Los Angeles, 1956 (Sanford Roth)

Westport, Connecticut, 1986 (Paul Newman)

Los Angeles, 1958 (Gene Lesser)

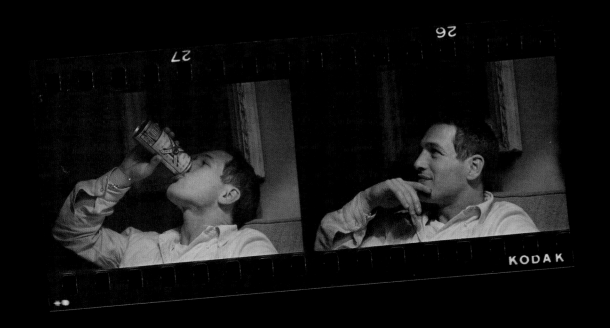

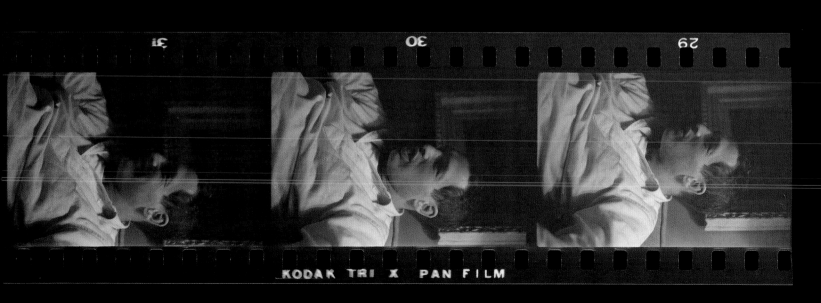

Chateau Marmont, Los Angeles, 1960 (Stewart Stern)

Thursday

Aprìes-la-telephone —

Darling —

We just spoke so... There's nothing to talk about in terms of events and The Chateau has not furnished any paper to write on and it's eleven twenty and my eyeball bags will be out in full bloom tomorrow morning and I haven't even looked at the script, but it occurred That I didn't really say goodnight — and sleep-well and bon voyage and all That other stuff That I should have said so I decided to write and say goodnight and sleep well and how you're the only person I ever looked at while They was sleeping That I could ever have The feeling That I loved and That I wanted to say goodnight to Three Thousand miles away and sleep well and bon voyage even Though I had just spoken on The telephone and The Chateau didn't furnish any paper to write on so goodnight anyway and don't Think That I wouldn't have written more except I'm running out of paper and I just spoke to you on

goodnight and it rattled around in my conscience. Then I went & got something to write it on. It begs this to be rained on while performance be cause I love you so There... I love you. The telephone except to say goodnight & forthwith

32   To Joanne, 1955 (Jerri Graham)

Soundstage recording session for *Paris Blues*, Studios de Boulogne, Boulogne-Billancourt, Hauts-de-Seine, 1960 (Sam Shaw)

Southern Vermont, 1956 (Stewart Stern)

Southern Vermont, 1956 (Stewart Stern)

38

PLUS X FILM

12 11 10

X FILM KODAK SAFETY FILM

X FILM

19 18

Southern Vermont, 1956 (Stewart Stern)

"The thing I resent about this sex-symbol thing is that writers create these sexy, flamboyant, aggressive characters who might have nothing to do with who you really are under the skin. You don't always have Tennessee Williams around to write glorious lines for you." —*Paul Newman*

La rue d'Orchampt, Montmartre, while filming *Paris Blues*, 1960–61 (Philippe Le Tellier)

"There's always room for a tree house, but you really have to think about it, because like everything else, if you don't think it out there's no point."
—*Paul Newman*

On honeymoon, Connaught Hotel, London, 1958

"Paul is not only a great actor—and that's all I can do, is act—he can write, he can produce and direct, race cars and run corporations, and he's a pretty good husband, too." —*Joanne Woodward*

On set while filming *From the Terrace*, 20th Century Fox Studios, Los Angeles, 1960

Westport, Connecticut, 1965 (Bruce Davidson

Beverly Hills, 1962 (Stewart Stern)

"I can see Joanne sitting quietly and knitting, but her mind is still snapping like a grasshopper." —*Paul Newman*

Saugatuck River, Westport, Connecticut, 1978 (Joanne Woodward)

Westport, Connecticut, 2000 (Wayne Saville)

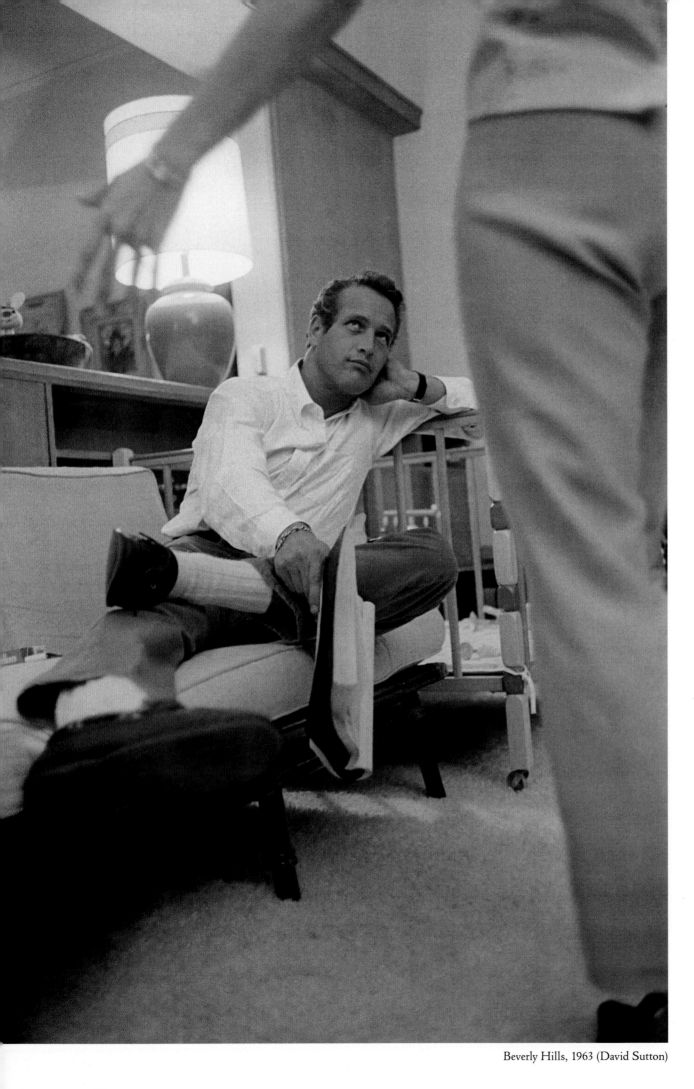

Beverly Hills, 1963 (David Sutton)

Bateau Mouche, Paris, 1960 (Sam Shaw)

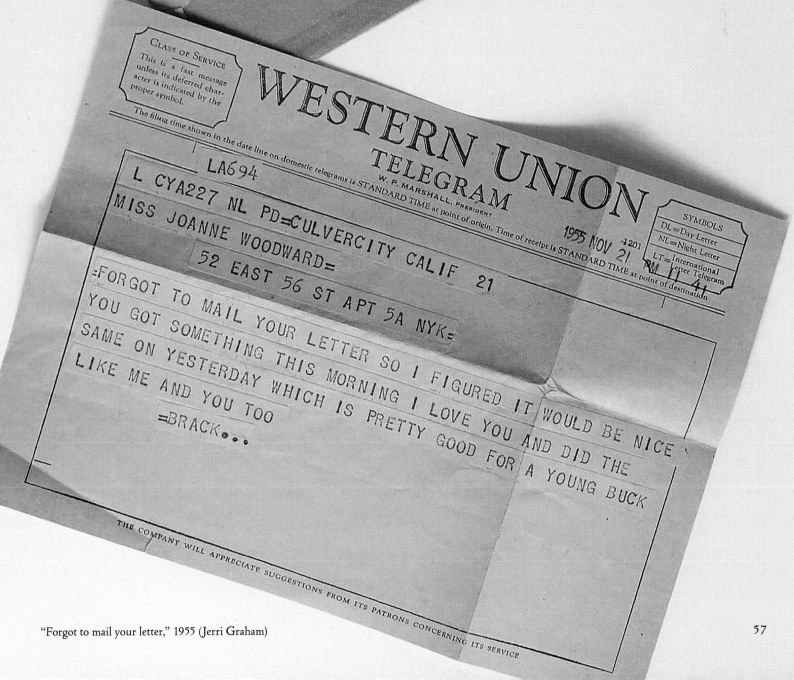

"Forgot to mail your letter," 1955 (Jerri Graham)

Château de Maintenon, Maintenon, Eure-et-Loir, 1960 (Paul Newman)

East Village, New York, 1959 (Gordon Parks)

Breakfast in Montmartre, 1960 (Philippe Le Tellier)

"I looked at a painting at a gallery on Madison Avenue that I really liked and wanted to buy for Joanne, but I just didn't know if it was good enough for her. If I brought it home, just on my own taste, I was afraid to think what she'd think. More than anything, I didn't want her to be disappointed in me." —*Paul Newman*

"No one sings like Woodward, or acts like Woodward, or bitches like Woodward or kisses like Woodward or talks like Woodward, or talks as long as Woodward, or wipes water out of her eyes like Woodward, or smiles like Woodward or cusses like Woodward. No one is as theatrical as Woodward, or changes like Woodward, or listens like Woodward, or laughs or cries or hiccups or nuthin' like Woodward. You is a special, a super, an absolutely unbeatable wench and I love you."
—*Paul Newman*

Paris, 1958 (Pierre Vauthey)

"Joanne and I live between two worlds and are accepted by neither. It's just like Thomas Mann's story, 'Tonio Kröger.' The bourgeois think we're revolutionaries and the bohemians see that we have a lot of Jell-O and don't wear neckerchiefs and they think we're bourgeois." —*Paul Newman*

Soundstage recording session for *Paris Blues*, Studios de Boulogne, Boulogne-Billancourt, Hauts-de-Seine, 1960 (Sam Shaw)

With Sanford Roth's cat, Los Angeles, 1956 (Sanford Roth)

"I'm all in favor of a good screaming free-for-all every two or three months. It clears the air, gets rid of old grievances, and generally makes for a pleasant relationship." —*Paul Newman*

Beverly Hills, 1958 (Sid Avery)

"I thought Paul was grossly untalented when I first met him. I remember going to dinner with Kim Stanley, when we were all doing *Picnic* together in Cleveland, and saying to her 'God, it's a good thing Paul Newman is handsome, because he certainly can't act.'" —*Joanne Woodward*

Beverly Hills, 1963 (David Sutton)

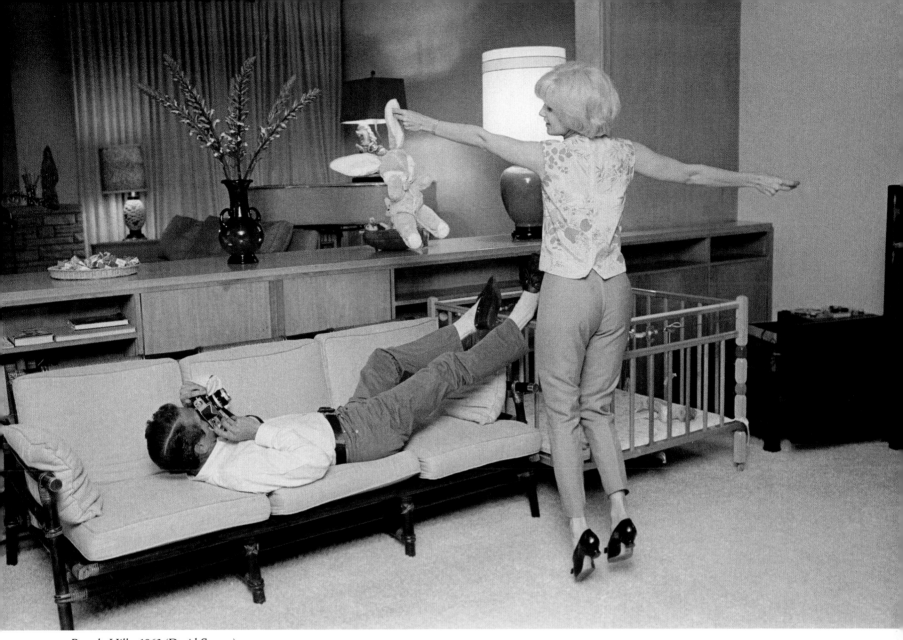

Beverly Hills, 1963 (David Sutton)

Westport, Connecticut, 1963 (Philippe Halsman)

"I don't like to talk about acting. It's very private. An actor is like a magician. You don't give away your secrets. That doesn't mean there isn't a lot going on before you face the camera or a live audience. I just don't talk about acting, and I don't talk about my sex life." —*Joanne Woodward*

On set with the script for *The Three Faces of Eve*, 20th Century Fox Studios, Los Angeles, 1956 (George Rinhart)

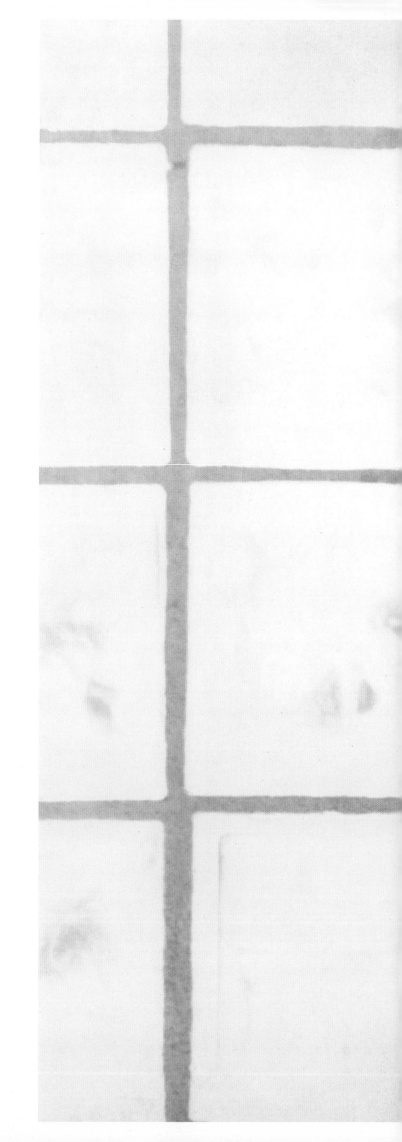

Los Angeles, 1958

"I got my Oscar when I was really young and it probably wasn't legitimate because I really think Oscars should mean more in terms of being for a body of work than one single performance. But I loved it, because my daydream had always been, when I was a little girl, to win an Oscar. And so, I was young enough to really feel marvelous about it." —*Joanne Woodward*

Beverly Hills, 1960

Academy Award for Best Actress in *The Three Faces of Eve*, RKO Pantages Theatre, Los Angeles, 1958 (Ralph Crane)

"Every time I get into an argument with Joanne about cooking or how to launder shirts, she just shakes her Oscar at me, and I'm dead in the water." —*Paul Newman*

84

With Oscar and "Noscar," Beverly Hills, 1958 (Sid Avery)

SURFBOARD
RENTALS. 1 HR
2 HR. MINIMUM

On location while filming *Winning*, Los Angeles, 1969

On location while filming *Winning*, Los Angeles, 1969

On break while filming *Exodus*, Protarus, Cyprus, 1960

On break while filming *Exodus*, Protarus, Cyprus, 1960

"Stars are people who are immediately recognizable, who bring their own mystique, their own essence to whatever role they play. Paul is a star. I think I'm a character actress. Nobody recognizes me when I walk down the street. And I can have a hard time getting checks cashed." —*Joanne Woodward*

On set while filming *Paris Blues*, Studios de Boulogne, Boulogne-Billancourt, Hauts-de-Seine, 1960 (Sam Shaw)

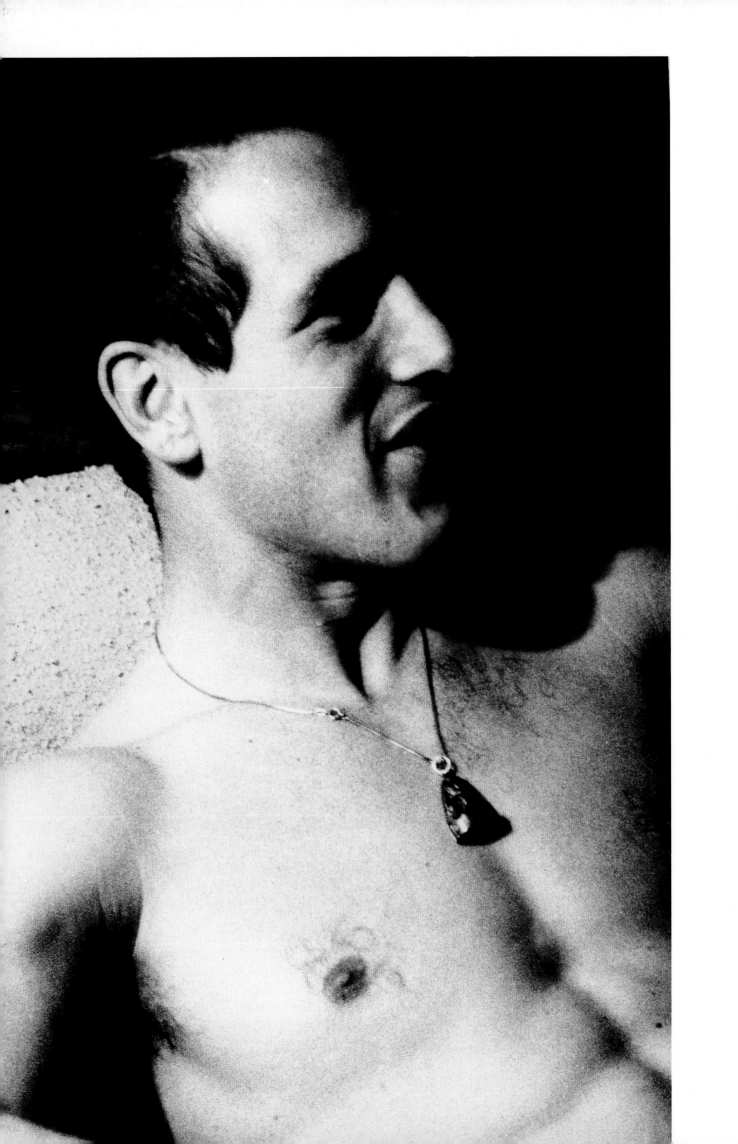

New York, 1957 (Philippe Halsman)

El Rancho Hotel, Las Vegas, 1958 (Stewart Stern)

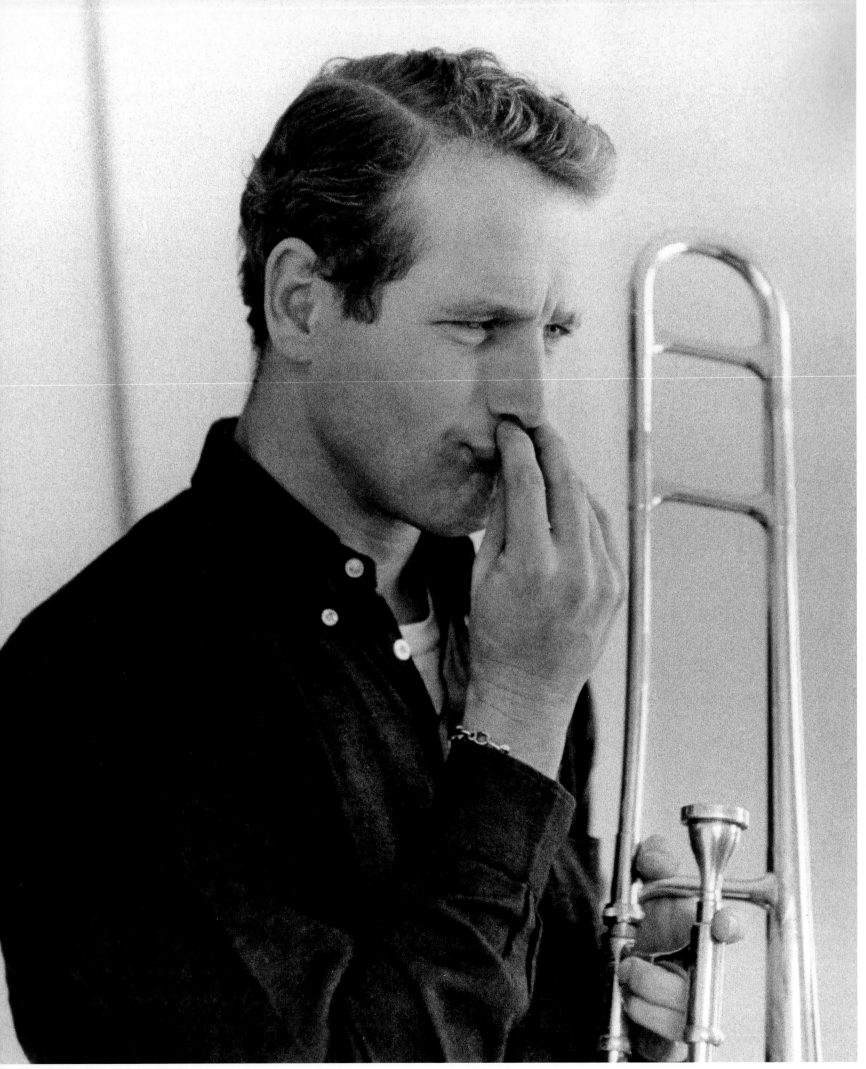

La rue d'Orchampt, Montmartre, while filming *Paris Blues*, 1960

On location while filming *No Down Payment*, Los Angeles, 1957 (Roger Marshutz)

Production still for *A New Kind of Love*, Paramount Studios, Los Angeles, 1963

Westport, Connecticut, 1963 (Philippe Halsman)

On break while filming *Exodus*, Dolphin House Hotel, Shavei Zion, Israel, 1960 (Leo Fuchs)

"Martha Graham used to say to us that you can create a character physically, and it's true, because when I'm acting, my physical appearance is totally important to me—how my hair is, what my clothes are, how my character walks and the way she speaks. I tend to work from the outside in, rather than from the inside out, which is totally opposed to all the training I've had from Sandy Meisner." —*Joanne Woodward*

"The Faces of Joanne," *Esquire*, September 1957 (Milton H. Greene)

New York, 1957

Tear sheet from "The Faces of Joanne," *Esquire*, September 1957 (Richard Avedon)

THE
FACES
OF
JOANNE

Joanne
Woodward,
portraying
variously
the
docile,
the
flirtatious,
and
the
mature
personalities
of
an
emotionally
disturbed
woman
in
a
new
film,
"The
Three
Faces
of
Eve,"

RICHARD AVEDON

107

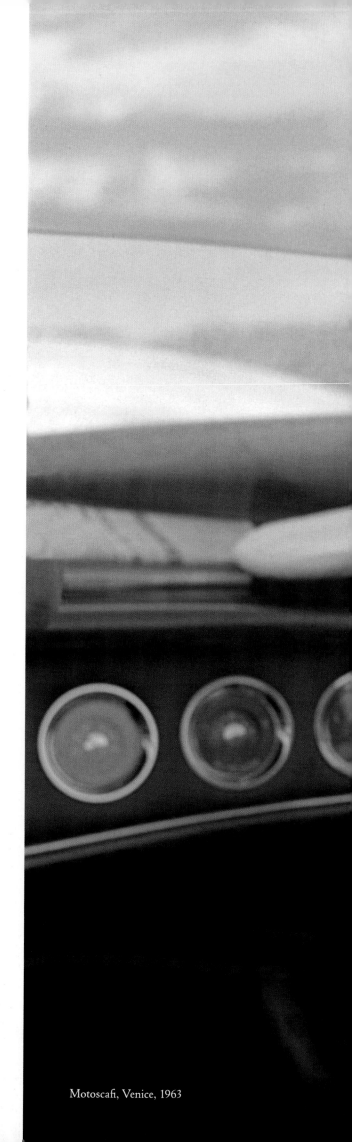

"I had no natural gift to be anything—not an athlete, not an actor, not a writer, not a director, or a painter of garden porches—not anything. So, I've worked really hard, because nothing ever came easily to me." —*Paul Newman*

Motoscafi, Venice, 1963

Love letters and telegrams, 1955–57 (Jerri Graham)

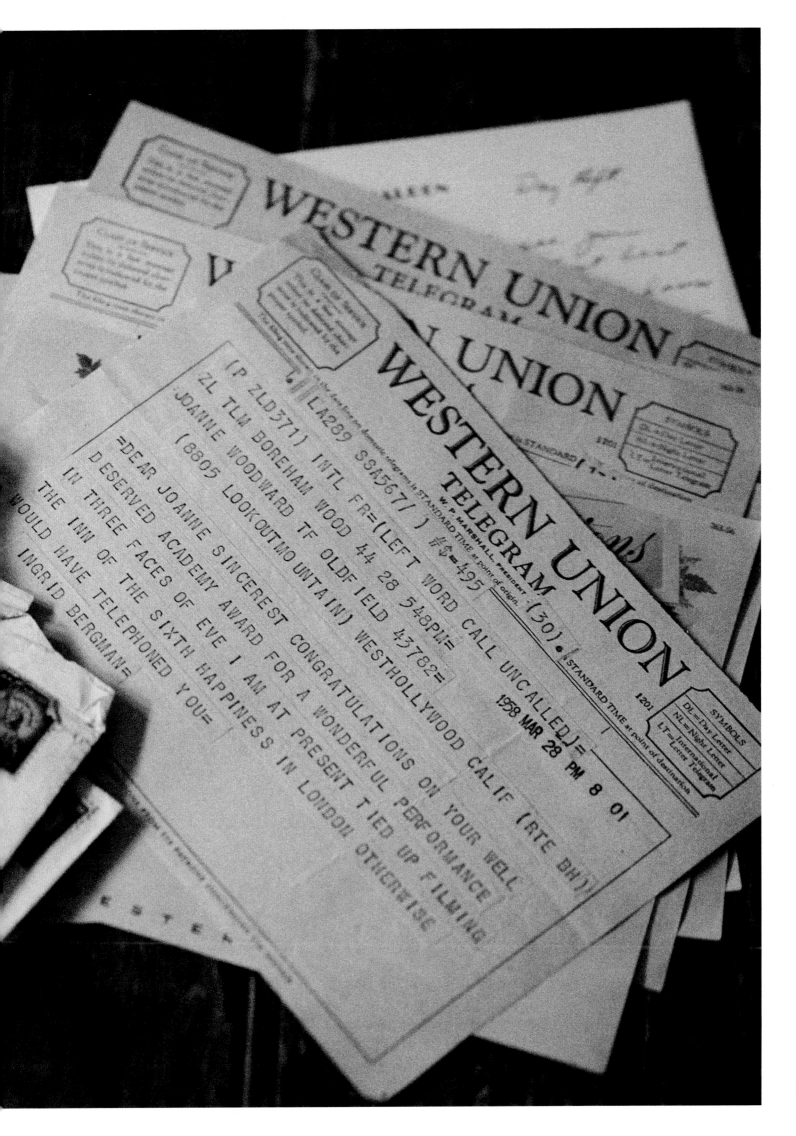

WESTERN UNION
TELEGRAM
W. P. MARSHALL, PRESIDENT

(P ZLD371) IWTL FR=(LEFT WORD CALL UNCALLED)=
ZL TLW BOREHAM WOOD 44 28 548PM=
JOANNE WOODWARD TF OLDFIELD 43782=
(8805 LOOKOUTMOUNTAIN) WESTHOLLYWOOD CALIF (RTE BH)=

=DEAR JOANNE SINCEREST CONGRATULATIONS ON YOUR WELL
DESERVED ACADEMY AWARD FOR A WONDERFUL PERFORMANCE
IN THREE FACES OF EVE I AM AT PRESENT TIED UP FILMING
THE INN OF THE SIXTH HAPPINESS IN LONDON OTHERWISE
WOULD HAVE TELEPHONED YOU=
INGRID BERGMAN=

LA289 SSA567( ) #$=495

1958 MAR 28 PM 8 01

1201

Beverly Hills, 1958

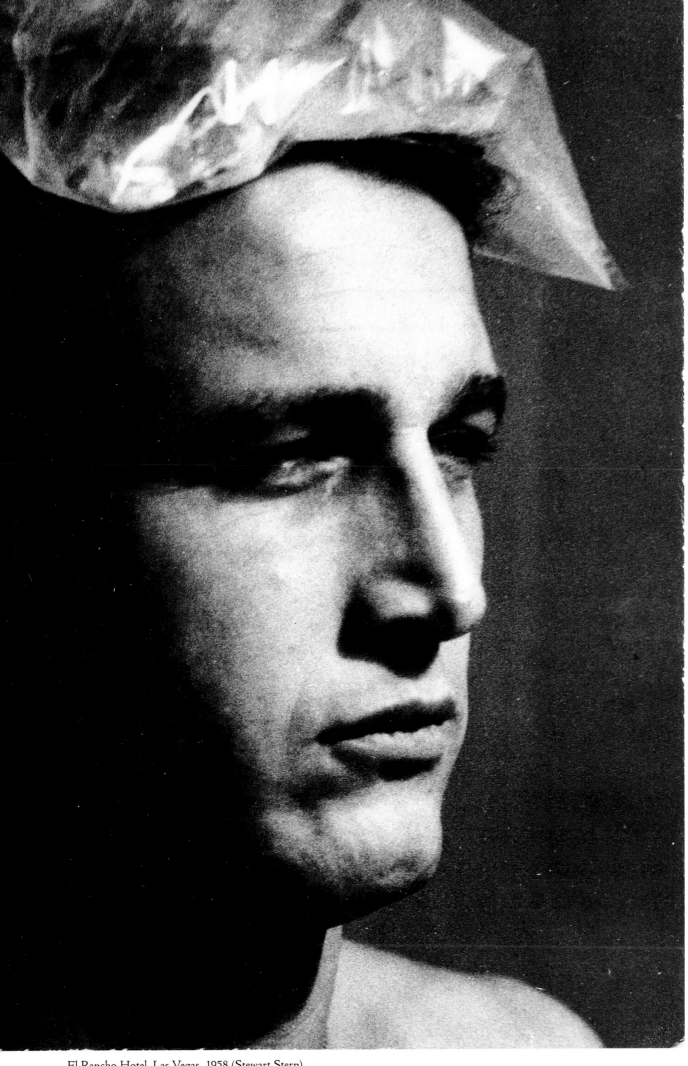

El Rancho Hotel, Las Vegas, 1958 (Stewart Stern)

Reading the script for *Baby Want a Kiss*, with author James Costigan and director Frank Corsaro, Westport, Connecticut, 1963 (Philippe Halsman)

Westport, Connecticut, 1963 (Philippe Halsman)

Westport, Connecticut, 1963 (Philippe Halsman)

Westport, Connecticut, 1963 (Philippe Halsman)

The Bahamas, 1967

Los Angeles, 1962

"I don't really understand Paul's acting technique but then he really doesn't understand mine either. He's so clear about what he's going to do before he does it. I can't do that." —*Joanne Woodward*

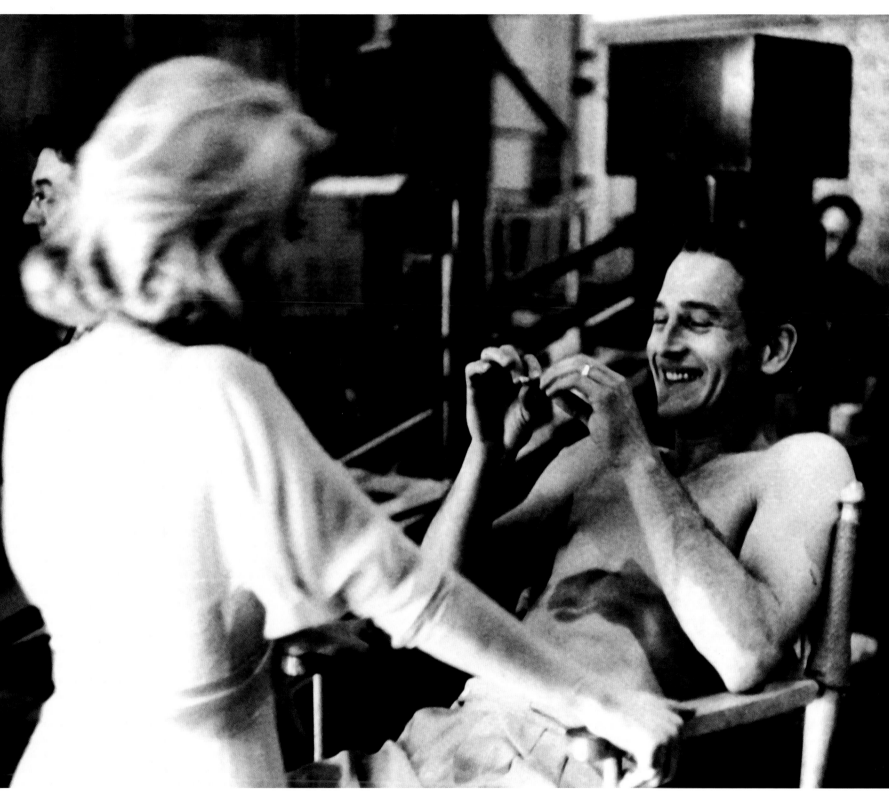

On set while filming *From the Terrace*, 20th Century Fox Studios, Los Angeles, 1960

On set while filming *From the Terrace*, 20th Century Fox Studios, Los Angeles, 1960 (Lawrence Schiller)

New York, 1957 (Philippe Halsman)

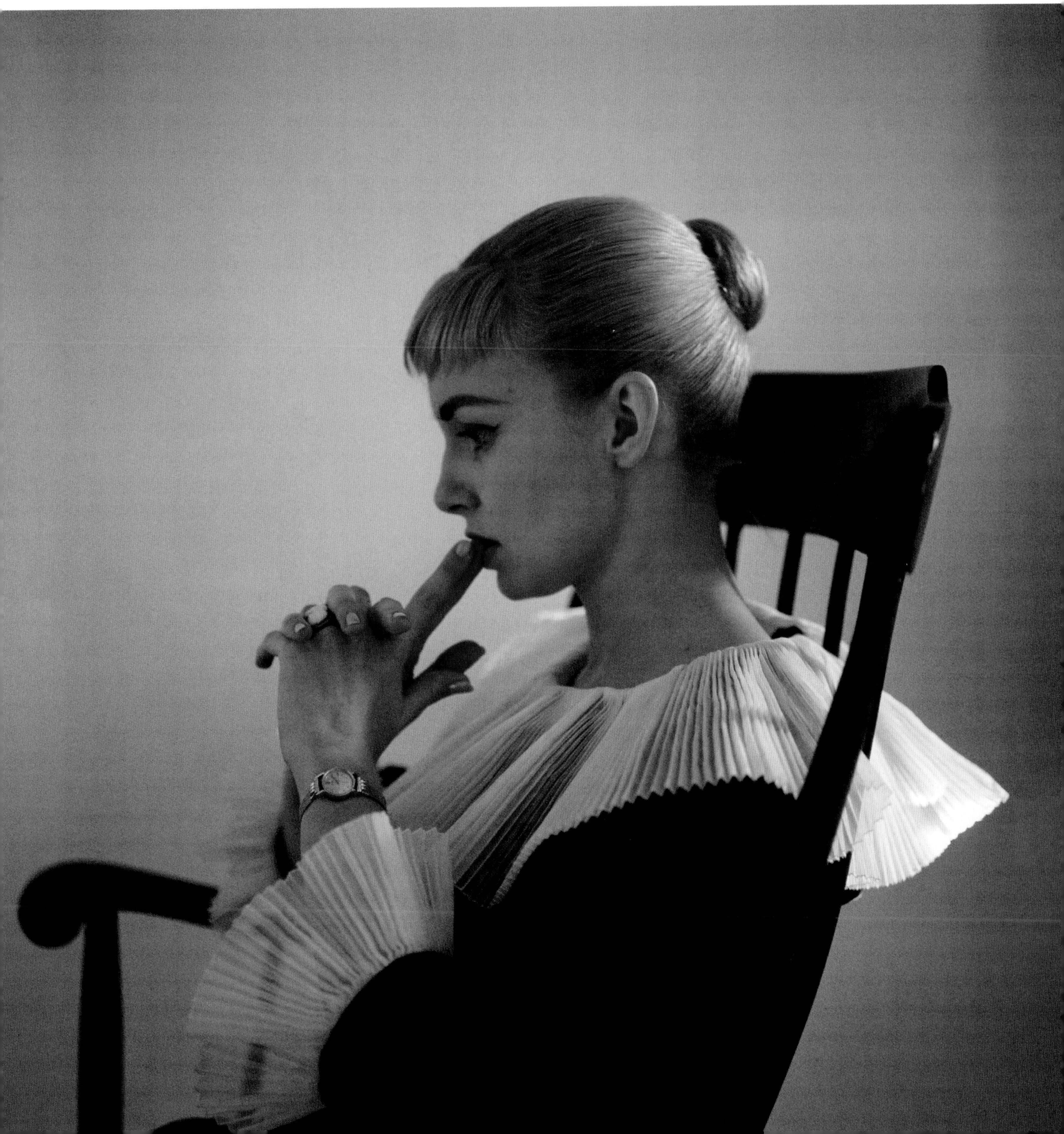

On set while filming *Paris Blues*, Studios de Boulogne, Boulogne-Billancourt, Hauts-de-Seine, 1960 (Philippe Le Tellier)

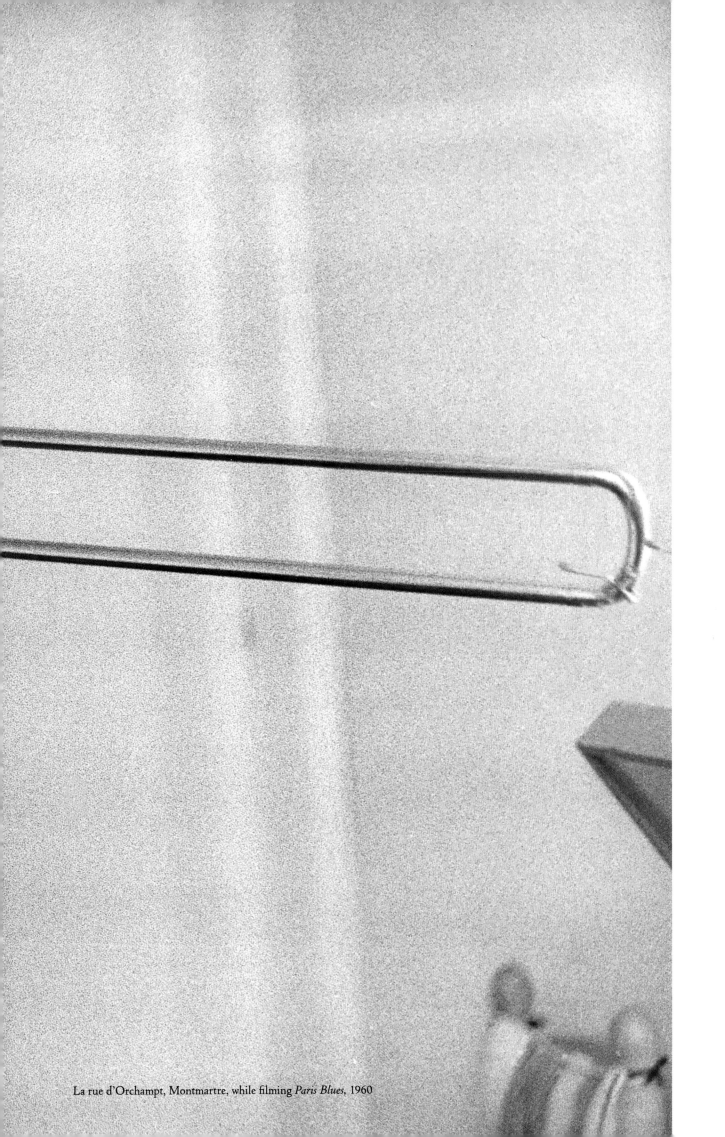

La rue d'Orchampt, Montmartre, while filming *Paris Blues*, 1960

On break while filming *The Long, Hot Summer*, Jackson, Louisiana, 1958

Chateau Marmont, Los Angeles, 1960 (Stewart Stern)

"Newman's luck. It's allowed me to take chances, to take risks. To get close to a lot of edges without falling off." —*Paul Newman*

On the Warner lot while filming *The Left Handed Gun*, Los Angeles, 1958 (John R. Hamilton)

"When an actor knows what they're doing you
don't see the work." —*Joanne Woodward*

Soundstage recording session for *Paris Blues*, Studios de Boulogne, Boulogne-Billancourt, Hauts-de-Seine, 1960 (Sam Shaw)

Westport, Connecticut, 2023 (Jerri Graham)

137

Greenwich Village, New York, 1961 (A. Louis Goldman)

"Paul is more beautiful than
I am, but he makes me feel like
a sex bomb."
—*Joanne Woodward*

On location while filming *Sweet Bird of Youth*, Los Angeles, 1962

On set while filming *Paris Blues*, Studios de Boulogne, Boulogne-Billancourt, Hauts-de-Seine, 1960 (Sam Shaw)

144

"One day when I was filming *The Stripper* I ran into Marilyn Monroe in the studio commissary, dressed, as I was, in my 'Marilyn Monroe' outfit with my 'Marilyn Monroe' hair and everything. And I didn't know what to say or do, but she did such a wonderful thing, because we just ran smack into each other—and I only knew her slightly—and I kind of went up in my register to a very breathy voice and said 'Hello, Marilyn,' which I didn't mean to do but I couldn't help it, and she went 'Hello, Joanne' in that same breathy voice. And then both of us started to laugh, which was very nice because she obviously saw what I was up to but took it the way I intended, which was as a compliment, as an homage." —*Joanne Woodward*

On set while filming *The Stripper*, 20th Century Fox Studios, Los Angeles, 1963

Dressing room on set while filming *The Stripper*, 20th Century Fox Studios, Los Angeles, 1963 (David Sutton)

Dressing room on set while filming *The Stripper*, 20th Century Fox Studios, Los Angeles, 1963

Beverly Hills, 1963 (David Sutton)

KODAK TRI X PAN FILM

→11

→12

Chateau Marmont, Los Angeles, 1960 (Stewart Stern)

"I check my pulse, and if I can find it,
I know I've got a chance." —*Paul Newman*

EKG reading, 1961 (Jerri Graham)

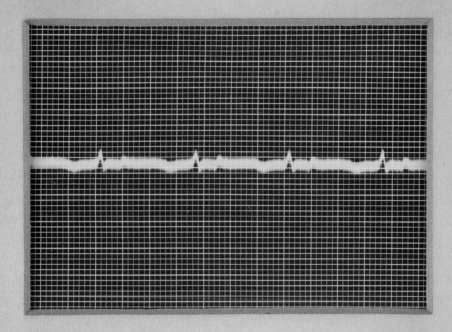

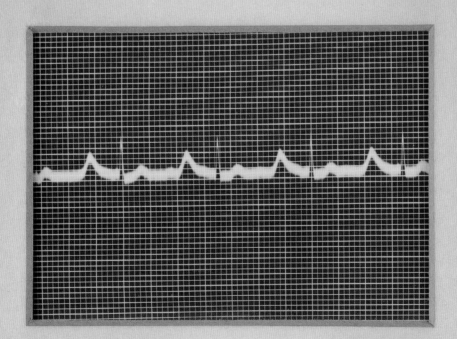

Lover —
You can tell by the murmurs
and the palpitations that it's
devoted! xxx PL

New York, 1957 (Philippe Halsman)

"I miss your sweet, gentle, non-aggressive, non-oblique, high-chested soul. At any rate I don't want to give you the impression that I miss you—or even like you—" —*Paul Newman*

Beverly Hills, 1960 (John Engstead)

The Parthenon, Athens, 1962

On set while filming *Paris Blues*, Studios de Boulogne, Boulogne-Billancourt, Hauts-de-Seine, 1960 (Sam Shaw)

"Joanne and I have had difficult, body-bending confrontations, but we haven't surrendered. I've packed up and left a few times, and then I realize I have no place to go and then I'm back in ten minutes. Ultimately, I think we both delight in watching the progression. And we laugh a lot."

—*Paul Newman*

"In those early days Paul mesmerized me, but after a while he went through a kind of metamorphosis that I can only say it's as if nothing succeeds like success, because I don't think Paul was very good until he became successful, and then he just got better and better. And he never settled for being just one thing. He never settled for just being a movie star." —*Joanne Woodward*

On location while filming *The Left Handed Gun*, Columbia Ranch, Burbank, California, 1958

El Rancho Hotel, Las Vegas, 1958 (Stewart Stern)

El Rancho Hotel, Las Vegas, 1958 (Stewart Stern)

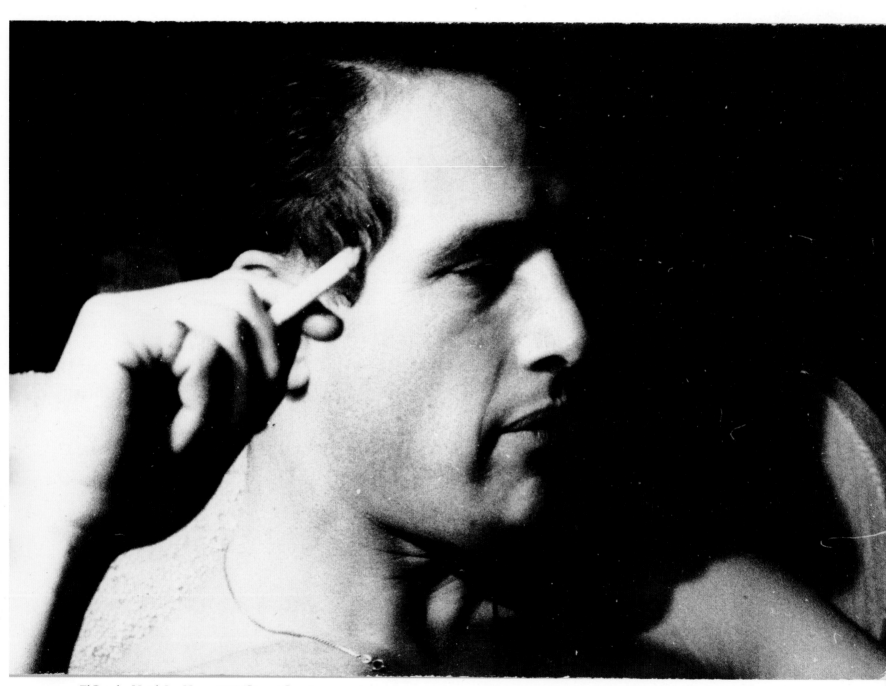

El Rancho Hotel, Las Vegas, 1958 (Stewart Stern)

On location while filming *The Long, Hot Summer*, Plantation Village Studios, Jackson, Louisiana, 1958 (Gene Lesser)

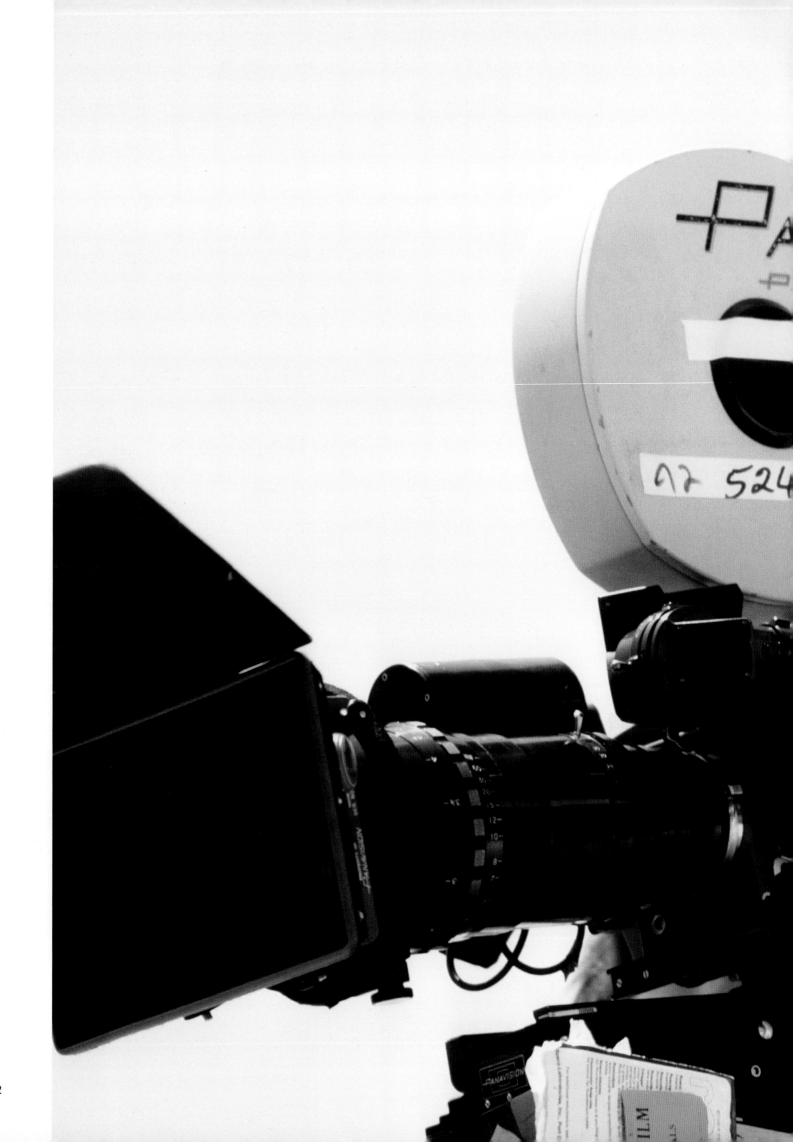

On location while directing *Harry & Son*, Lake Worth, Florida, 1984 (Steve Schapiro)

Sidetracked at a qualifying run for the SCCA Trans-Am Championship Opener, Moroso Motorsports Park, Jupiter, Florida, 1984

On location while filming *Winning*, Riverside International Raceway, Moreno Valley, California, 1969 (Lawrence Schiller)

"In acting, you have to do it wrong in order to do it right, and the same is true in car racing." —*Paul Newman*

"Joanne has always given me unconditional support in all my choices and endeavors, and that includes my race car driving, which she deplores. To me, that's love."
—*Paul Newman*

On location while filming *Winning*, Riverside International Raceway, Moreno Valley, California, 1969 (Lawrence Schiller)

On location while directing *The Effect of Gamma Rays on Man-in-the-Moon Marigolds*, Bridgeport, Connecticut, 1972

"Newman's first law is that it's useless to put your brakes on when you are upside down." —*Paul Newman*

Lime Rock Park, Lakeville, Connecticut, 1979

On location while filming *Once Upon a Wheel*, Ontario Motor Speedway, Ontario, California, 1971

"I think what describes Joanne's feeling about my racing was a headline once in the *New York Post* that said 'Newman Escapes Death, Joanne Furious.'" —*Paul Newman*

On location while filming *Winning*, Riverside International Raceway, Moreno Valley, California, 1969 (Lawrence Schiller)

On location while filming *Winning*, Riverside International Raceway, Moreno Valley, California, 1969 (Lawrence Schiller)

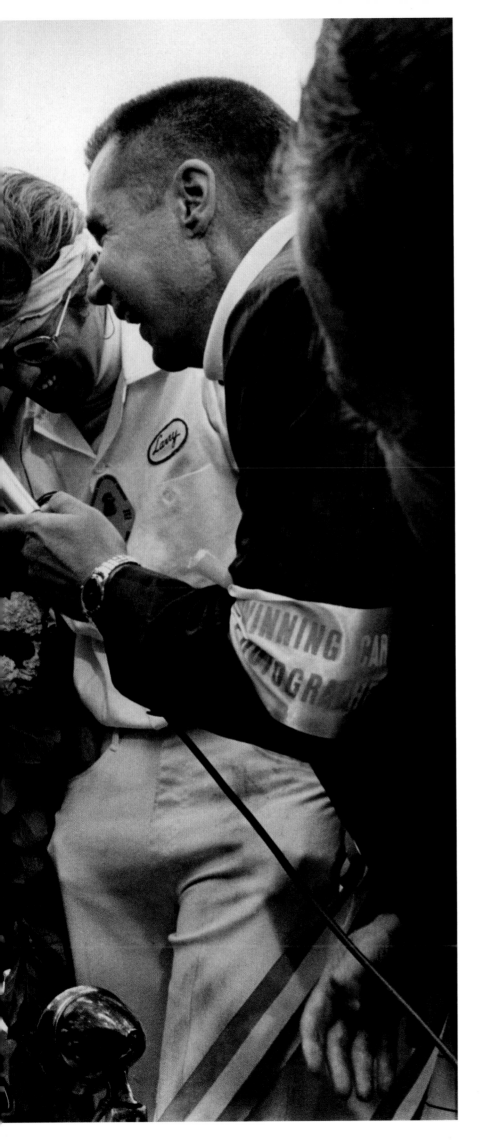

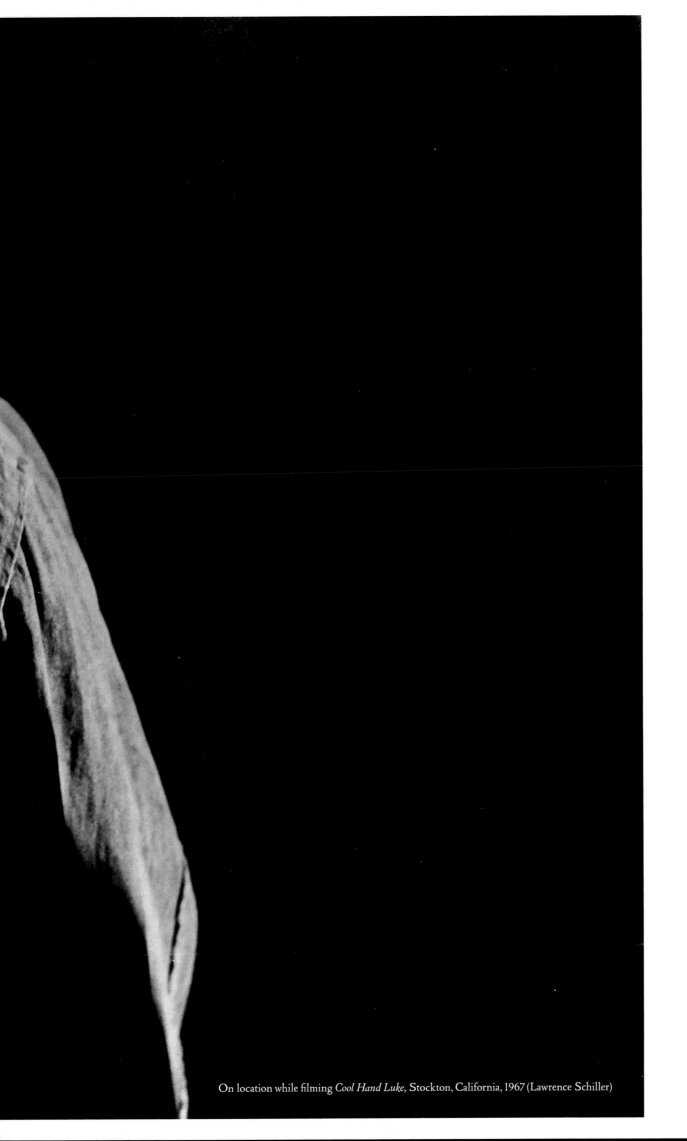

On location while filming *Cool Hand Luke*, Stockton, California, 1967 (Lawrence Schiller)

"If you have no enemies, you have no character." —*Paul Newman*

On location while filming *The Outrage*, Sierrita Mountains, Arizona, 1964

KODAK PLUS X PAN FILM

KODAK SAFETY FILM

KODAK PLUS X PAN FILM

KODAK SAFETY FILM

KODAK PLUS X PAN FILM

"This is just to let you know the pictures on the wall are crooked, that there are light bulbs that don't work in the lamps, that the handle is off the door to the sauna, that I had no pot to melt my butter in for popcorn last night… that it is gray out, that there is a lady behind us in her apartment parading around without any brassiere. What are you up to?"

—*Paul Newman*

Beverly Hills, 1962 (Stewart Stern)

Beverly Hills, 1962 (Stewart Stern)

"Don't kid your material." —*Joanne Woodward*

On location while filming *The Life and Times of Judge Roy Bean*, Sonoran Desert, Arizona, 1972

"There's some pretty strange element about taking yourself seriously. You have to take yourself seriously enough so that you work well in your craft. And you certainly don't belittle it. But all of the peripheral stuff—the sense of royalty, the sense of entitlement—I think you've got to be very careful that you don't believe your own publicity." —*Paul Newman*

Installation of the Official Poster of the 66th Cannes Film Festival, Palais des Festivals et des Congrès, Cannes, 2013 (Valery Hache)

Cannes Film Festival, Cannes, 1973

202

Democratic National Convention, Chicago, 1968

"Being an actor does not excuse you from being a citizen." —*Paul Newman*

"I'm not intellectually astute enough to discuss, for instance, politics, nor would I want to. I don't want to put myself in the position of being someone who knows what they're talking about unless I really did. And in most cases I probably don't. Paul, on the other hand, is intellectually knowledgeable about the subjects that he discusses and the causes he believes in, and he has every right to talk about them." —*Joanne Woodward*

On set while filming *WUSA*, New Orleans, 1970 (Lawrence Schiller)

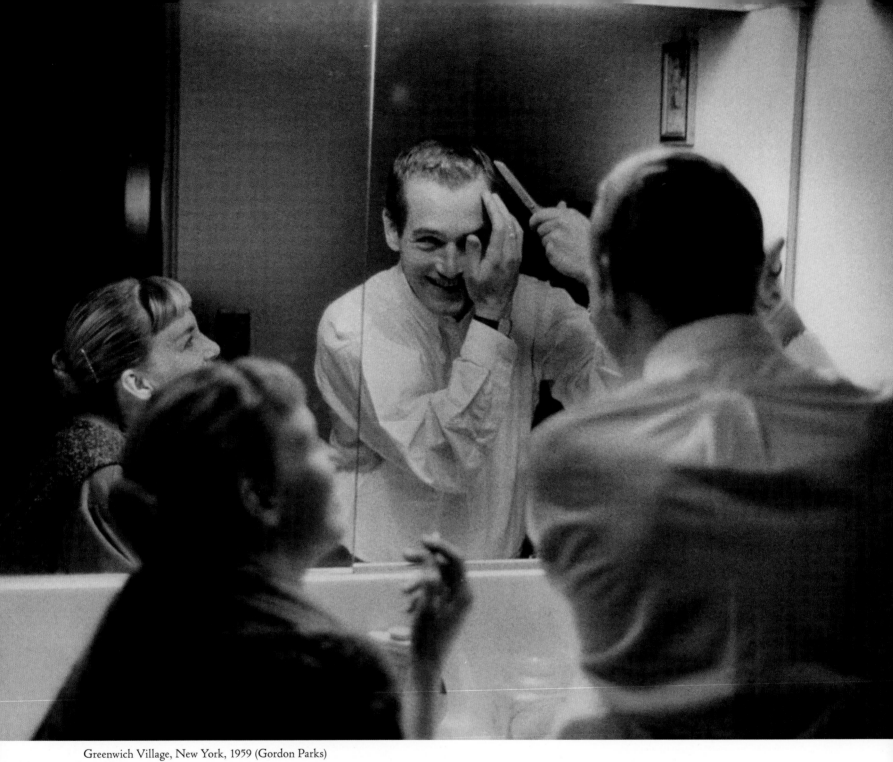

Greenwich Village, New York, 1959 (Gordon Parks)

Recording a public service announcement for the Muscular Dystrophy Association, New York, 1963 (Philippe Halsman)

208

"Sexiness wears thin after a while and beauty fades,
but to be married to a man who makes you laugh every day,
now that's a real treat." —*Joanne Woodward*

Westport, Connecticut, 1965 (David Sutton)

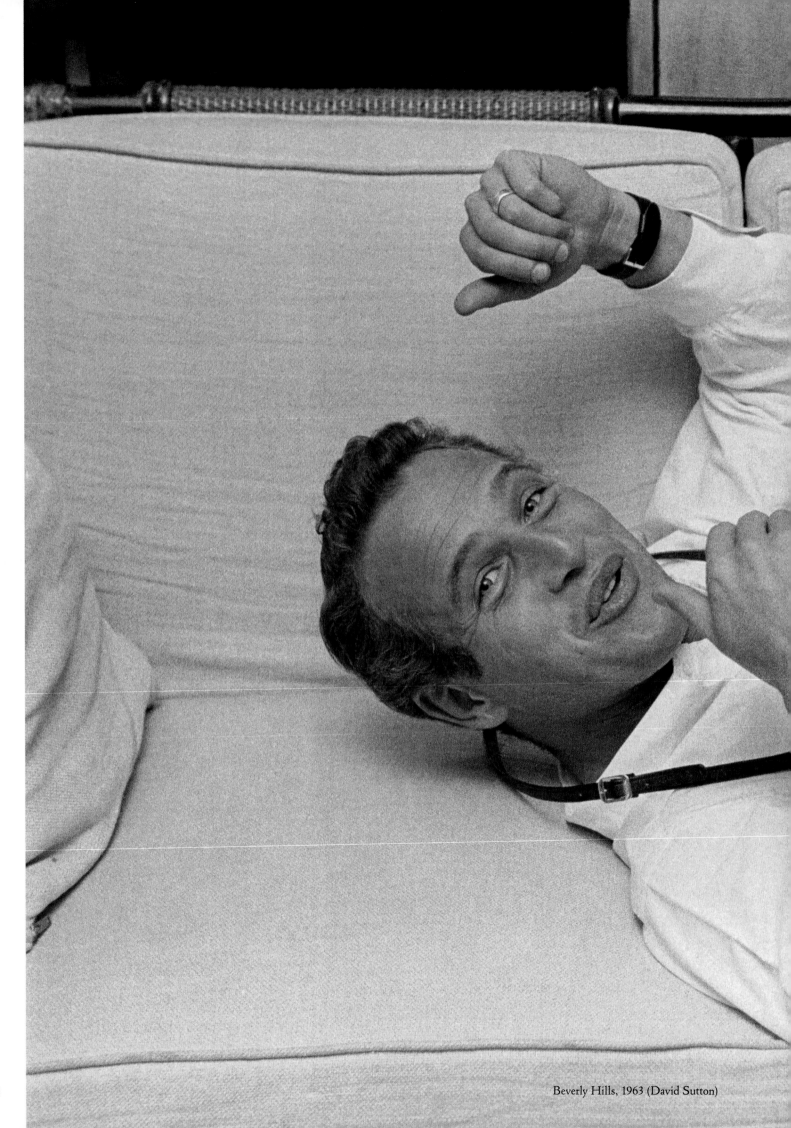

212   Beverly Hills, 1963 (David Sutton)

Westport, Connecticut, 1965 (David Sutton)

Westport, Connecticut, 1965 (David Sutton)

216

On the lot of 20th Century Fox Studios while filming *Rally Round the Flag, Boys!*, Los Angeles, 1958 (Sid Avery)

On location while filming *Hud*, Claude, Texas, 1962 (Bradley Smith)

Production still for *A New Kind of Love*, Paramount Studios, Los Angeles, 1963

"Joanne brought me a script for *A New Kind of Love*, and, after looking it over, I told her I thought it was the worst piece of crap I'd ever read. She started weeping and told me 'I have raised our children, and helped raise your children, and now I bring you a film where I get to wear gorgeous costumes and dress up and have fun and you won't do it.' And so I said, I've changed my mind, it's the best thing I've ever read."

—*Paul Newman*

"I wish I wasn't as private a person as I am and I wish Joanne wasn't as private a person as she is. Because you see people who kind of bathe in those very public situations, who go straight into the teeth of their audience. I've always been uncomfortable like that. I try to move crabwise into restaurants chewing on match covers. The only reservation that I have is really in myself." —*Paul Newman*

On location while filming *Sweet Bird of Youth*, Los Angeles, 1962

On location while filming *Cool Hand Luke*, San Joaquin Valley, California, 1967

On location while filming *Cool Hand Luke*, Stockton, California, 1967 (Lawrence Schiller)

225

With Christine White in The Actors Studio, 1955 (Roy Schatt)

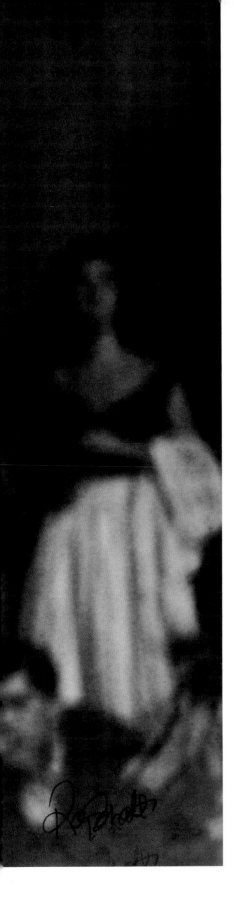

"It was really only after I got to The Actors Studio and watched the corps of actors there—Karl Malden, Kim Stanley, Barbara Baxley, Eli Wallach, Geraldine Page, the whole list of them—to watch these people in action, the observation of them, gave me more I think than from anything else." —*Paul Newman*

Westport, Connecticut, 1968 (Milton H. Greene)

La rue d'Orchampt, Montmartre, while filming *Paris Blues*, 1960

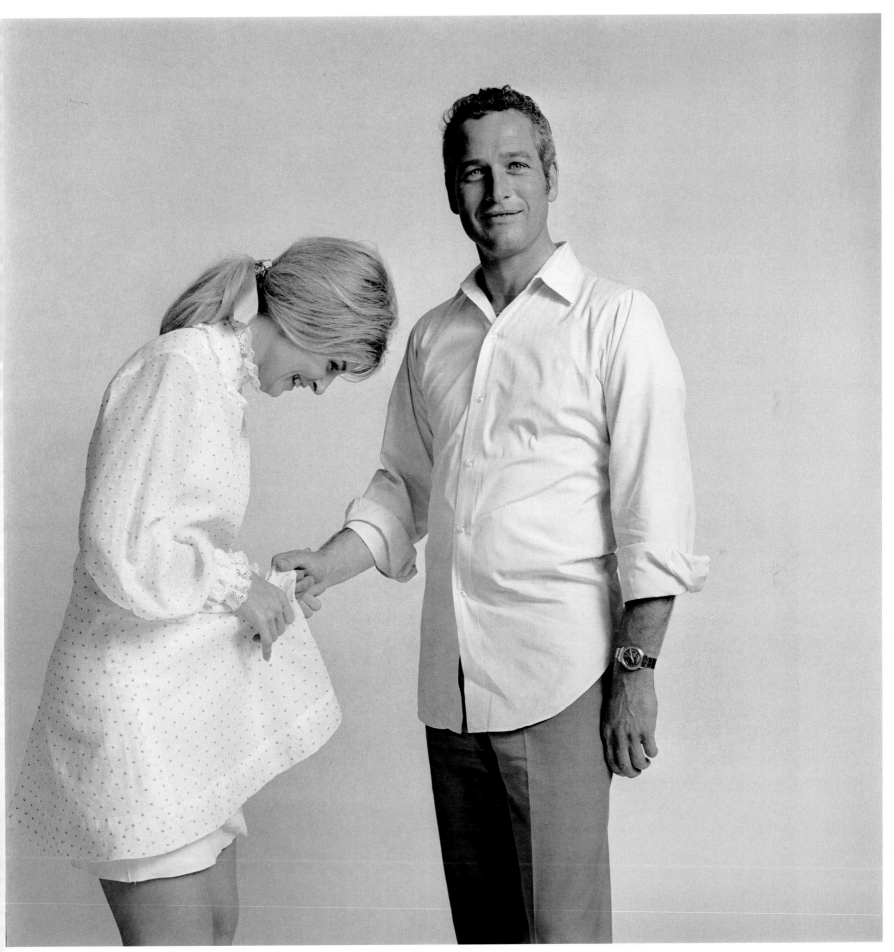

On set while filming *WUSA*, New Orleans, 1970 (Lawrence Schiller)

On set while filming *From the Terrace*, 20th Century Fox Studios, Los Angeles, 1960 (Lawrence Schiller)

On set while filming *From the Terrace*, 20th Century Fox Studios, Los Angeles, 1960 (Lawrence Schiller)

"I could only dance with one person, that was Joanne. I could never dance with anyone else." —*Paul Newman*

On location while directing *Rachel, Rachel*, Danbury, Connecticut, 1968

Grauman's Chinese Theatre, Hollywood, 1963 (Lawrence Schiller)

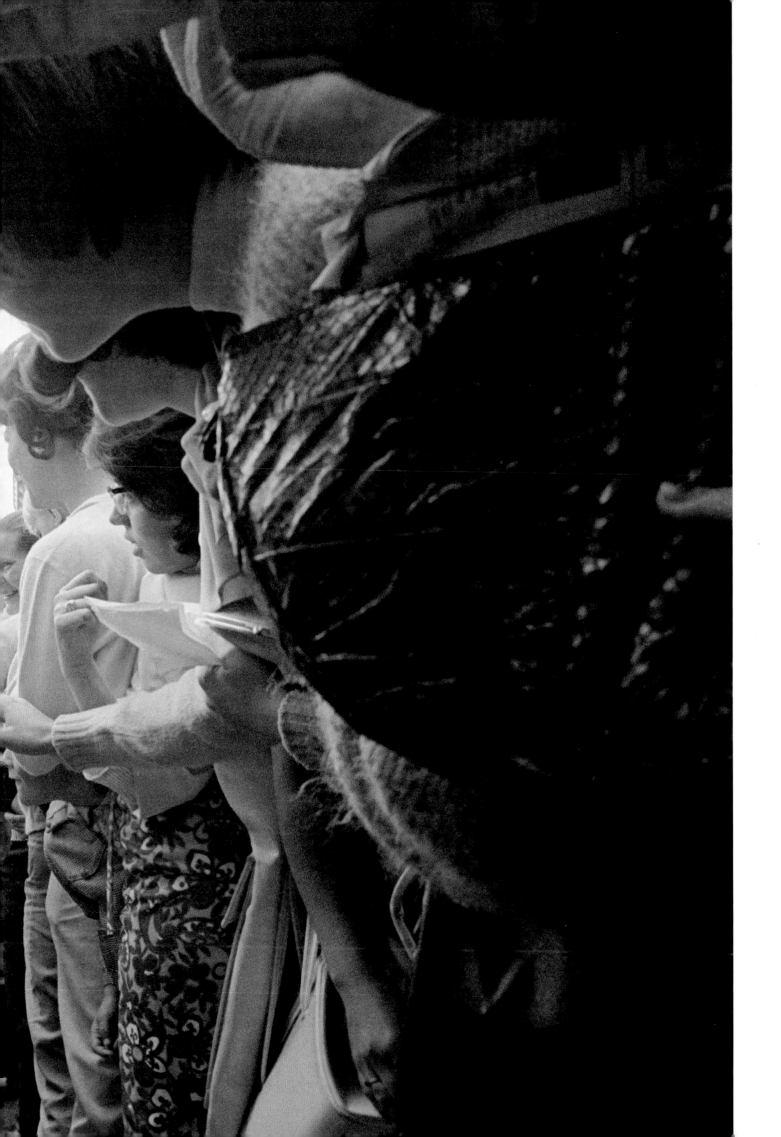

240

Grauman's Chinese Theatre, Hollywood, 1963 (Lawrence Schiller)

Grauman's Chinese Theatre, Hollywood, 1963 (Lawrence Schiller)

Grauman's Chinese Theatre, Hollywood, 1963 (Lawrence Schiller)

On location while filming *Somebody Up There Likes Me*, New York, 1956

On location while filming *The Long, Hot Summer*, Clinton, Louisiana, 1958

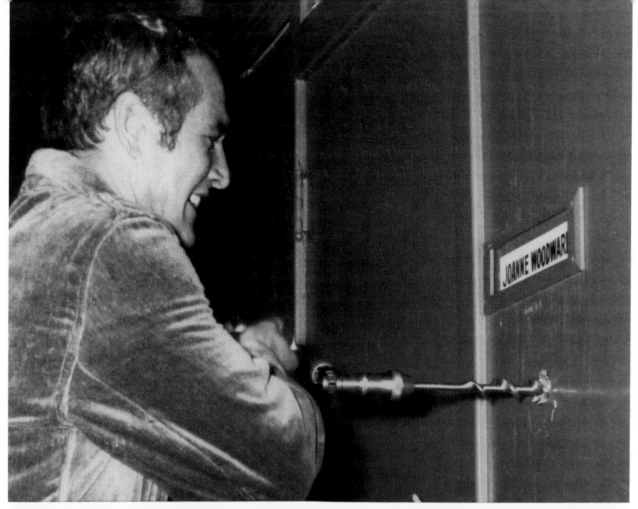

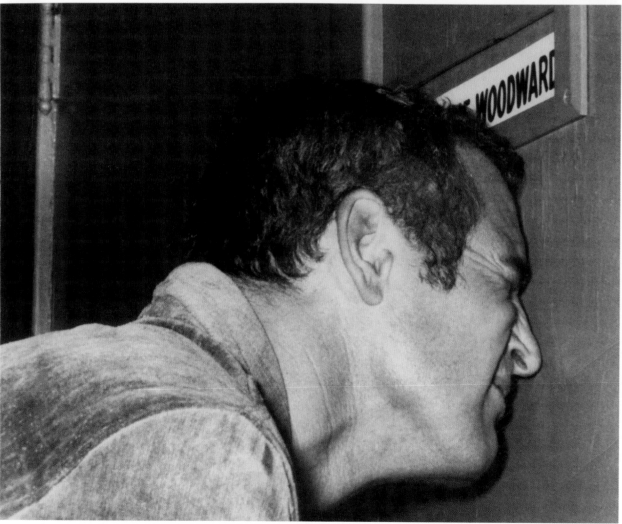

On the set of *WUSA*, New Orleans, 1970

On the lot of 20th Century Fox Studios while filming *Rally Round the Flag, Boys!*, Los Angeles, 1958 (Sid Avery)

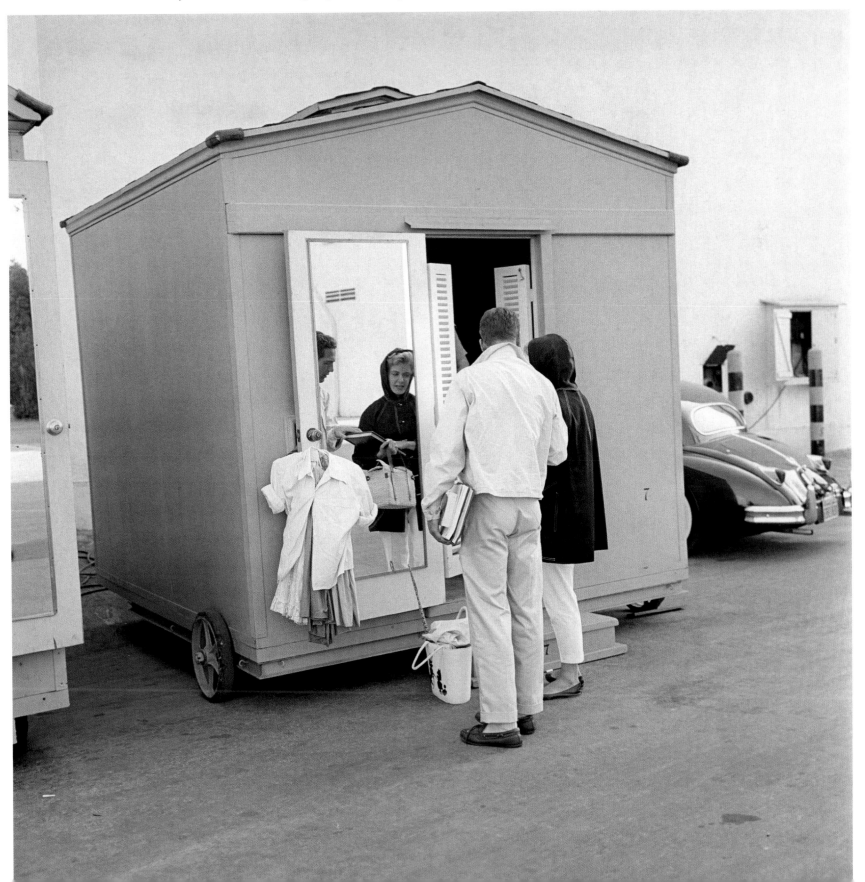

Fundraiser, Hollywood, 1963

"In any art form, it doesn't matter whether it's painting or writing or dance or whatever, the real joy is to go from the technique you've learned on to the thing that works for you. You take what you can from your training, then you go on to find your method, and that's your technique."

—*Joanne Woodward*

The Actors Studio, 1955 (Roy Schatt)

"Just to watch Joanne listening is a course in acting itself." —*Paul Newman*

On set while filming *Paris Blues*, Studios de Boulogne, Boulogne-Billancourt, Hauts-de-Seine, 1960 (Sam Shaw)

PHOTOGRAPHY INDEX

Dust jacket   Chateau Marmont, Los Angeles, 1960. Photographs by Stewart Stern,
               © Joanne Woodward Newman

Endpapers   Beverly Hills, 1963. Photographs by David Sutton, © David Sutton, courtesy MPTV Images

8   My sister Nell, Beverly Hills, 1960. Photograph by Paul Newman, © Joanne Woodward Newman

11   Westport, Connecticut, 1988. Photograph by Paul Newman, © Joanne Woodward Newman

12   Beverly Hills, 1967. Photograph by Joanne Woodward, © Joanne Woodward Newman

15   Downstairs bedroom door, Westport, Connecticut, 2023. Photograph by Jerri Graham,
               © Joanne Woodward Newman

16   Saugatuck River, Westport, Connecticut, 1965. Photograph by Bruce Davidson,
               © Bruce Davidson/Magnum Photos

18   El Rancho Hotel, Las Vegas, 1958. Photograph by Stewart Stern, © Joanne Woodward Newman

18   Westport, Connecticut, 2023. Photograph by Jerri Graham, © Joanne Woodward Newman

19   El Rancho Hotel, Las Vegas, 1958. Photograph by Stewart Stern, © Joanne Woodward Newman

20   New York, 1956. Photograph by Paul Newman, © Joanne Woodward Newman

21   New York, 1955. Photograph by Joanne Woodward, © Joanne Woodward Newman

22   Westport, Connecticut, 2023. Photograph by Jerri Graham, © Joanne Woodward Newman

24   On break while filming *The Long, Hot Summer,* Jackson, Louisiana, 1958. © Joanne Woodward Newman

25   On break while filming *The Long, Hot Summer,* Jackson, Louisiana, 1958. © Joanne Woodward Newman

27   With Sanford Roth's cat at Griffith Park Zoo, Los Angeles, 1956. Photographs by Sanford Roth,
               © Sanford Roth, courtesy MPTV Images

28   Westport, Connecticut, 1986. Photograph by Paul Newman, © Joanne Woodward Newman

29   Los Angeles, 1958. Photograph by Gene Lesser, Zuma Press

30   Chateau Marmont, Los Angeles, 1960. Photographs by Stewart Stern, © Joanne Woodward Newman

32   To Joanne, 1955. Photograph by Jerri Graham, 2023, © Joanne Woodward Newman

33   Soundstage recording session for *Paris Blues*, Studios de Boulogne, Boulogne-Billancourt, Hauts-de-Seine, 1960. Photograph by Sam Shaw, © 1960–2023 Shaw Family Archives

34   Southern Vermont, 1956. Photograph by Stewart Stern, © Joanne Woodward Newman

36   Southern Vermont, 1956. Photographs by Stewart Stern, © Joanne Woodward Newman

37   Southern Vermont, 1956. Photographs by Stewart Stern, © Joanne Woodward Newman

38   Southern Vermont, 1956. Photographs by Stewart Stern, © Joanne Woodward Newman

40   Southern Vermont, 1956. Photograph by Stewart Stern, © Joanne Woodward Newman

41   Southern Vermont, 1956. Photographs by Stewart Stern, © Joanne Woodward Newman

43   Westport, Connecticut, 1962. New York Daily News Archive via Getty Images

44   La rue d'Orchampt, Montmartre, while filming *Paris Blues*, 1960–61. Photograph by Philippe Le Tellier, Paris Match Archive via Getty Images

46   On honeymoon, Connaught Hotel, London, 1958. Manchester Daily Express via Getty Images

49   On set while filming *From the Terrace*, 20th Century Fox Studios, Los Angeles, 1960. Globe Photos, Zuma Press

50   Westport, Connecticut, 1965. Photographs by Bruce Davidson, © Bruce Davidson/Magnum Photos

52   Beverly Hills, 1962. Photograph by Stewart Stern, © Joanne Woodward Newman

53   Saugatuck River, Westport, Connecticut, 1978. Photograph by Joanne Woodward, © Joanne Woodward Newman

53   Westport, Connecticut, 2000. Photograph by Wayne Saville, © Joanne Woodward Newman

54   Beverly Hills, 1963. Photograph by David Sutton, © David Sutton, courtesy MPTV Images

55   Beverly Hills, 1963. Photograph by David Sutton, © David Sutton, courtesy MPTV Images

56   Bateau Mouche, Paris, 1960. Photograph by Sam Shaw, © 1960–2023 Shaw Family Archives

57   "Forgot to mail your letter," 1955. Photograph by Jerri Graham, 2023, © Joanne Woodward Newman

58   Château de Maintenon, Maintenon, Eure-et-Loir, 1960. Photograph by Paul Newman, © Joanne Woodward Newman

60   East Village, New York, 1959. Photograph by Gordon Parks, LIFE Picture Collection, courtesy Shutterstock

61   Breakfast in Montmartre, 1960. Photograph by Philippe Le Tellier, Paris Match Archive via Getty Images

63   Paris, 1958. Photograph by Pierre Vauthey, Sigma Collection via Getty Images

65   Soundstage recording session for *Paris Blues*, Studios de Boulogne, Boulogne-Billancourt, Hauts-de-Seine, 1960. Photograph by Sam Shaw, © 1960–2023 Shaw Family Archives

66   With Sanford Roth's cat, Los Angeles, 1956. Photograph by Sanford Roth, © Sanford Roth, courtesy MPTV Images

69   Beverly Hills, 1958. Photograph by Sid Avery, © Sid Avery, courtesy MPTV Images

71   Beverly Hills, 1963. Photograph by David Sutton, © David Sutton, courtesy MPTV Images

72   Beverly Hills, 1963. Photograph by David Sutton, © David Sutton, courtesy MPTV Images

73   Beverly Hills, 1963. Photograph by David Sutton, © David Sutton, courtesy MPTV Images

74   "Women I Like to Sleep With," Westport, Connecticut, 2023. Photograph by Jerri Graham, © Joanne Woodward Newman

75   Westport, Connecticut, 1963. Photograph by Philippe Halsman, © Philippe Halsman Estate 2023

77   On set with the script for *The Three Faces of Eve*, 20th Century Fox Studios, Los Angeles, 1956. Photograph by George Rinhart, 20th Century Fox Film Corporation, courtesy Everett Collection

78   Los Angeles, 1958. Everett Collection

81   Beverly Hills, 1960. Globe Photos, Zuma Press

82   Academy Award for Best Actress in *The Three Faces of Eve*, RKO Pantages Theatre, Los Angeles, 1958. Photograph by Ralph Crane, LIFE Picture Collection, courtesy Shutterstock

83   Academy Award for Best Actress in *The Three Faces of Eve*, RKO Pantages Theatre, Los Angeles, 1958. Photograph by Ralph Crane, LIFE Picture Collection, courtesy Shutterstock

84   With Oscar and "Noscar," Beverly Hills, 1958. Photograph by Sid Avery, © Sid Avery, courtesy MPTV Images

86   On location while filming *Winning*, Los Angeles, 1969. Bettmann Archive via Getty Images

88   On location while filming *Winning*, Los Angeles, 1969. Bettmann Archive via Getty Images

89   On break while filming *Exodus*, Protarus, Cyprus, 1960. Mondadori Portfolio Premium via Getty Images

90   On break while filming *Exodus*, Protarus, Cyprus, 1960. Mondadori Portfolio Premium via Getty Images

92   On set while filming *Paris Blues*, Studios de Boulogne, Boulogne-Billancourt, Hauts-de-Seine, 1960. Photograph by Sam Shaw, © 1960–2023 Shaw Family Archives

94   El Rancho Hotel, Las Vegas, 1958. Photograph by Stewart Stern, © Joanne Woodward Newman

95   New York, 1957. Photograph by Philippe Halsman, © Philippe Halsman Estate 2023

96   La rue d'Orchampt, Montmartre, while filming *Paris Blues*, 1960. Courtesy SIPA USA

97   On location while filming *No Down Payment*, Los Angeles, 1957. Photograph by Roger Marshutz, © Roger Marshutz, courtesy MPTV Images

98   Production still for *A New Kind of Love*, Paramount Studios, Los Angeles, 1963. Everett Collection

100   Westport, Connecticut, 1963. Photograph by Philippe Halsman, © Philippe Halsman Estate 2023

102   On break while filming *Exodus*, Dolphin House Hotel, Shavei Zion, Israel, 1960. Photograph by Leo Fuchs, © Leo Fuchs, courtesy MPTV Images

103   On break while filming *Exodus*, Dolphin House Hotel, Shavei Zion, Israel, 1960. Photograph by Leo Fuchs, © Leo Fuchs, courtesy MPTV Images

105   "The Faces of Joanne," *Esquire*, September 1957. Photograph by Milton H. Greene, © 2023 Joshua Greene

106   New York, 1957. © Joanne Woodward Newman

107   Tear sheet from "The Faces of Joanne," *Esquire*, September 1957. Photograph by Richard Avedon, © 2023 The Richard Avedon Foundation

108   Motoscafi, Venice, 1963. Archivio Cameraphoto Epoche via Getty Images

110   Love letters and telegrams, 1955–57. Photograph by Jerri Graham, 2023, © Joanne Woodward Newman

112   Beverly Hills, 1958. © Joanne Woodward Newman

113   El Rancho Hotel, Las Vegas, 1958. Photograph by Stewart Stern, © Joanne Woodward Newman

114   Reading the script for *Baby Want a Kiss*, with author James Costigan and director Frank Corsaro, Westport, Connecticut, 1963. Photograph by Philippe Halsman, © Philippe Halsman Estate 2023

116   Westport, Connecticut, 1963. Photographs by Philippe Halsman, © Philippe Halsman Estate 2023

118   Westport, Connecticut, 1963. Photograph by Philippe Halsman, © Philippe Halsman Estate 2023

119   Westport, Connecticut, 1963. Photographs by Philippe Halsman, © Philippe Halsman Estate 2023

120   The Bahamas, 1967. © Joanne Woodward Newman

121   Los Angeles, 1962. © Joanne Woodward Newman

123   On set while filming *From the Terrace*, 20th Century Fox Studios, Los Angeles, 1960.
Globe Photos, Zuma Press

124   On set while filming *From the Terrace*, 20th Century Fox Studios, Los Angeles, 1960. Photograph
by Lawrence Schiller, © Lawrence Schiller, all rights reserved

125   New York, 1957. Photograph by Philippe Halsman, © Philippe Halsman Estate 2023

126   On set while filming *Paris Blues*, Studios de Boulogne, Boulogne-Billancourt, Hauts-de-Seine, 1960.
Photograph by Philippe Le Tellier, Paris Match Archive via Getty Images

128   La rue d'Orchampt, Montmartre, while filming *Paris Blues*, 1960. Courtesy SIPA USA

130   On break while filming *The Long, Hot Summer*, Jackson, Louisiana, 1958. © Joanne Woodward Newman

131   Chateau Marmont, Los Angeles, 1960. Photograph by Stewart Stern, © Joanne Woodward Newman

133   On the Warner lot while filming *The Left Handed Gun*, Los Angeles, 1958. Photograph by
John R. Hamilton, © John R. Hamilton/Trunk Archive

135   Soundstage recording session for *Paris Blues*, Studios de Boulogne, Boulogne-Billancourt,
Hauts-de-Seine, 1960. Photograph by Sam Shaw, © 1960–2023 Shaw Family Archives

136   Westport, Connecticut, 2023. Photograph by Jerri Graham, © Joanne Woodward Newman

138   Greenwich Village, New York, 1961. Photograph by A. Louis Goldman, Photo Researchers
via Getty Images

139   Greenwich Village, New York, 1961. Photograph by A. Louis Goldman, Photo Researchers
via Getty Images

140   Greenwich Village, New York, 1961. Photograph by A. Louis Goldman, Photo Researchers
via Getty Images

142   Zuma Beach, Malibu, 1957. Photograph by Ulrich Strauss, Globe Photos, Zuma Press

143   On location while filming *Sweet Bird of Youth*, Los Angeles, 1962. Mary Evans Picture Library,
        AF Archive, Everett Collection

144   On set while filming *Paris Blues*, Studios de Boulogne, Boulogne-Billancourt, Hauts-de-Seine, 1960.
        Photograph by Sam Shaw, © 1960–2023 Shaw Family Archives

147   On set while filming *The Stripper*, 20th Century Fox Studios, Los Angeles, 1963. 20th Century Fox
        Film Corporation, courtesy Everett Collection

148   Dressing room on set while filming *The Stripper*, 20th Century Fox Studios, Los Angeles, 1963.
        Photograph by David Sutton, © David Sutton, courtesy MPTV Images

149   Dressing room on set while filming *The Stripper*, 20th Century Fox Studios, Los Angeles, 1963.
        Globe Photos, Zuma Press

150   Beverly Hills, 1963. Photographs by David Sutton, © David Sutton, courtesy MPTV Images

151   Beverly Hills, 1963. Photographs by David Sutton, © David Sutton, courtesy MPTV Images

152   Chateau Marmont, Los Angeles, 1960. Photographs by Stewart Stern, © Joanne Woodward Newman

153   Chateau Marmont, Los Angeles, 1960. Photographs by Stewart Stern, © Joanne Woodward Newman

155   EKG reading, 1961. Photograph by Jerri Graham, 2023, © Joanne Woodward Newman

156   Westport, Connecticut, 1963. Photographs by Philippe Halsman, © Philippe Halsman Estate 2023

157   New York, 1957. Photograph by Philippe Halsman, © Philippe Halsman Estate 2023

159   Beverly Hills, 1960. Photograph by John Engstead, © John Engstead, courtesy MPTV Images

160   The Parthenon, Athens, 1962. © Joanne Woodward Newman

161   The Parthenon, Athens, 1962. © Joanne Woodward Newman

162   On set while filming *Paris Blues*, Studios de Boulogne, Boulogne-Billancourt, Hauts-de-Seine, 1960.
        Photographs by Sam Shaw, © 1960–2023 Shaw Family Archives

165   On location while filming *The Left Handed Gun*, Columbia Ranch, Burbank, California, 1958.
        Movie Star News, Zuma Press

166   El Rancho Hotel, Las Vegas, 1958. Photograph by Stewart Stern, © Joanne Woodward Newman

167   El Rancho Hotel, Las Vegas, 1958. Photograph by Stewart Stern, © Joanne Woodward Newman

168   Westport, Connecticut, 2023. Photograph by Jerri Graham, © Joanne Woodward Newman

169   El Rancho Hotel, Las Vegas, 1958. Photograph by Stewart Stern, © Joanne Woodward Newman

170   El Rancho Hotel, Las Vegas, 1958. Photograph by Stewart Stern, © Joanne Woodward Newman

171   On location while filming *The Long, Hot Summer,* Plantation Village Studios, Jackson, Louisiana, 1958. Photograph by Gene Lesser, Zuma Press

172   On location while directing *Harry & Son,* Lake Worth, Florida, 1984. Photograph by Steve Schapiro, Corbis Premium Historical via Getty Images

174   Sidetracked at a qualifying run for the SCCA Trans-Am Championship Opener, Moroso Motorsports Park, Jupiter, Florida, 1984. The Palm Beach Post, Zuma Press

176   On location while filming *Winning,* Riverside International Raceway, Moreno Valley, California, 1969. Photograph by Lawrence Schiller, © Lawrence Schiller, all rights reserved

178   On location while filming *Winning,* Riverside International Raceway, Moreno Valley, California, 1969. Photograph by Lawrence Schiller, © Lawrence Schiller, all rights reserved

179   On location while filming *Winning,* Riverside International Raceway, Moreno Valley, California, 1969. Photograph by Lawrence Schiller, © Lawrence Schiller, all rights reserved

180   On location while directing *The Effect of Gamma Rays on Man-in-the-Moon Marigolds,* Bridgeport, Connecticut, 1972. © Joanne Woodward Newman

181   Lime Rock Park, Lakeville, Connecticut, 1979. © Joanne Woodward Newman

182   On location while filming *Once Upon a Wheel,* Ontario Motor Speedway, Ontario, California, 1971. Everett Collection

185   On location while filming *Winning,* Riverside International Raceway, Moreno Valley, California, 1969. Photograph by Lawrence Schiller, © Lawrence Schiller, all rights reserved

186   On location while filming *Winning,* Riverside International Raceway, Moreno Valley, California, 1969. Photograph by Lawrence Schiller, © Lawrence Schiller, all rights reserved

188   On location while filming *Cool Hand Luke,* Stockton, California, 1967. Photograph by Lawrence Schiller, © Lawrence Schiller, all rights reserved

191   On location while filming *The Outrage,* Sierrita Mountains, Arizona, 1964. Everett Collection

192   Beverly Hills, 1962. Photographs by Stewart Stern, © Joanne Woodward Newman

194   Beverly Hills, 1962. Photograph by Stewart Stern, © Joanne Woodward Newman

195   Beverly Hills, 1962. Photograph by Stewart Stern, © Joanne Woodward Newman

197   On location while filming *The Life and Times of Judge Roy Bean*, Sonoran Desert, Arizona, 1972. Everett Collection

199   Installation of the Official Poster of the 66th Cannes Film Festival, Palais des Festivals et des Congrès, Cannes, 2013. Photograph by Valery Hache, Agence France-Presse via Getty Images

200   Cannes Film Festival, Cannes, 1973. Giribaldi via Getty Images

202   Democratic National Convention, Chicago, 1968. CBS Photo Archive via Getty Images

204   On set while filming *WUSA*, New Orleans, 1970. Photograph by Lawrence Schiller, © Lawrence Schiller, all rights reserved

206   Greenwich Village, New York, 1959. Photograph by Gordon Parks, LIFE Picture Collection, courtesy Shutterstock

207   Recording a public service announcement for the Muscular Dystrophy Association, New York, 1963. Photograph by Philippe Halsman, © Philippe Halsman Estate 2023

208   Westport, Connecticut, 1965. Photograph by David Sutton, © David Sutton, courtesy MPTV Images

209   Westport, Connecticut, 1965. Photograph by David Sutton, © David Sutton, courtesy MPTV Images

210   Westport, Connecticut, 1965. Photograph by David Sutton, © David Sutton, courtesy MPTV Images

211   Westport, Connecticut, 1965. Photograph by David Sutton, © David Sutton, courtesy MPTV Images

212   Beverly Hills, 1963. Photograph by David Sutton, © David Sutton, courtesy MPTV Images

214   Westport, Connecticut, 1965. Photograph by David Sutton, © David Sutton, courtesy MPTV Images

216   Westport, Connecticut, 1965. Photograph by David Sutton, © David Sutton, courtesy MPTV Images

217   Westport, Connecticut, 1965. Photograph by David Sutton, © David Sutton, courtesy MPTV Images

218   On the lot of 20th Century Fox Studios while filming *Rally Round the Flag, Boys!*, Los Angeles, 1958. Photograph by Sid Avery, © Sid Avery, courtesy MPTV Images

219   On location while filming *Hud*, Claude, Texas, 1962. Photograph by Bradley Smith, Corbis Premium Historical via Getty Images

220   Production still for *A New Kind of Love*, Paramount Studios, Los Angeles, 1963. Everett Collection

223   On location while filming *Sweet Bird of Youth*, Los Angeles, 1962. Everett Collection

224   On location while filming *Cool Hand Luke*, San Joaquin Valley, California, 1967. Glasshouse, Zuma Press

225 On location while filming *Cool Hand Luke*, Stockton, California, 1967. Photograph by Lawrence Schiller,

226 With Christine White in The Actors Studio, 1955. Photograph by Roy Schatt, courtesy Westwood Gallery, New York

228 Westport, Connecticut, 1968. Photographs by Milton H. Greene,

229 La rue d'Orchampt, Montmartre, while filming *Paris Blues*, 1960. Courtesy SIPA USA

230 On set while filming *WUSA*, New Orleans, 1970. Photographs by Lawrence Schiller,

231 On set while filming *WUSA*, New Orleans, 1970. Photograph by Lawrence Schiller,

232 On set while filming *From the Terrace*, 20th Century Fox Studios, Los Angeles, 1960. Photograph by Lawrence Schiller,

233 On set while filming *From the Terrace*, 20th Century Fox Studios, Los Angeles, 1960. Photographs by Lawrence Schiller,

234 On set while filming *From the Terrace*, 20th Century Fox Studios, Los Angeles, 1960. Photograph by Lawrence Schiller,

235 On set while filming *From the Terrace*, 20th Century Fox Studios, Los Angeles, 1960. Photograph by Lawrence Schiller,

236 On location while directing *Rachel, Rachel*, Danbury, Connecticut, 1968.

238 Grauman's Chinese Theatre, Hollywood, 1963. Photograph by Lawrence Schiller,

240 Grauman's Chinese Theatre, Hollywood, 1963. Photograph by Lawrence Schiller,

242 Grauman's Chinese Theatre, Hollywood, 1963. Photograph by Lawrence Schiller,

244 Grauman's Chinese Theatre, Hollywood, 1963. Photograph by Lawrence Schiller,

245 Grauman's Chinese Theatre, Hollywood, 1963. Photograph by Lawrence Schiller,

246 Grauman's Chinese Theatre, Hollywood, 1963. Photograph by Lawrence Schiller, © Lawrence Schiller, all rights reserved

248 On location while filming *Somebody Up There Likes Me*, New York, 1956. Sunset Boulevard, Corbis Premium Historical via Getty Images, and Globe Photos, Zuma Press

249 On location while filming *Somebody Up There Likes Me*, New York, 1956. Sunset Boulevard, Corbis Premium Historical via Getty Images, and Globe Photos, Zuma Press

250 On location while filming *The Long, Hot Summer*, Clinton, Louisiana, 1958. Globe Photos, Zuma Press

252 On the set of *WUSA*, New Orleans, 1970. © Joanne Woodward Newman

253 On the lot of 20th Century Fox Studios while filming *Rally Round the Flag, Boys!*, Los Angeles, 1958. Photograph by Sid Avery, © Sid Avery, courtesy MPTV Images

254 Fundraiser, Hollywood, 1963. Keystone-France via Getty Images

257 The Actors Studio, 1955. Photograph by Roy Schatt, © Estate of Roy Schatt, courtesy Westwood Gallery, New York

258 Beverly Hills, 1958. Photograph by Leonard McCombe, LIFE Picture Collection, courtesy Shutterstock

260 On set while filming *Paris Blues*, Studios de Boulogne, Boulogne-Billancourt, Hauts-de-Seine, 1960. Photograph by Sam Shaw, © 1960–2023 Shaw Family Archives

272 Westport, Connecticut, 2023. Photograph by Jerri Graham, © Joanne Woodward Newman

274 With Nell, Beverly Hills, 1960. Photograph by Stewart Stern, © Joanne Woodward Newman

280 With Nell, New York, 1959. Photograph by Paul Newman, © Joanne Woodward Newman

281 With Nell and Melissa, Westport, Connecticut, 1963. Photograph by Joanne Woodward, © Joanne Woodward Newman

282 With Susan, Stephanie, Nell, and Melissa, Beverly Hills, 1967. © Joanne Woodward Newman

Westport, Connecticut, 2023 (Jerri Graham)

273

With Nell, Beverly Hills, 1960 (Stewart Stern)

Joanne Woodward

(b. 1930)

Joanne Woodward is an American actor, director, producer, philanthropist, and social advocate. She was born in Thomasville, Georgia, in 1930 and was raised in the South. She graduated from Greenville High School in Greenville, South Carolina, in 1947, majored in drama at Louisiana State University from 1947 to 1949, and earned a Bachelor of Arts degree from Sarah Lawrence College in 1990.

In 1950, Woodward moved to New York City to study at The Actors Studio, and with Sanford Meisner and Martha Graham at the Neighborhood Playhouse School of the Theatre. During this time, Woodward appeared in numerous early live television dramatic anthology series, including *Tales of Tomorrow* (1952), *Goodyear Playhouse* (1952), *Robert Montgomery Presents* (1952–54), *Omnibus* (1952–55), *The Philco Television Playhouse* (1953), *You Are There* (1953–54), *Danger* (1954), *The Ford Television Theatre* (1954), *The Elgin Hour* (1954), *Lux Video Theatre* (1954), *Armstrong Circle Theatre* (1954), *Ponds Theatre* (1954–55), *Studio One* (1954–56), *Four Star Playhouse* (1954–56), *The Star and the Story* (1955), *Star Tonight* (1955), *The United States Steel Hour* (1955), *The 20th Century Fox Hour* (1955), *Kraft Theatre* (1955–56), *The Alcoa Hour* (1956), *General Electric Theatre* (1956), *Alfred Hitchcock Presents* (1956), and *Playhouse 90* (1958). Woodward also auditioned for roles on Broadway and understudied Janice Rule and Kim Stanley during the original production of William Inge's *Picnic* at the Music Box Theatre in 1953–54. Woodward's other Broadway and regional stage acting credits include *The Lovers* at the Martin Beck Theatre in 1956, *Baby Want a Kiss* at the Little Theatre in 1964, *Candida* at Kenyon Festival Theatre and Circle in the Square Theatre in 1981–83, *The Glass Menagerie* at Williamstown Theatre Festival and Long Wharf Theatre at New Haven in 1985–86, *Ghosts* with the River Arts Repertory at Woodstock in 1991, *The Waverly Gallery* at Williamstown in 1999, and *Ancestral Voices* at the Westport Country Playhouse in 2000. She also directed stage productions of *Golden Boy* at Williamstown in 1987, *Rocket to the Moon* at Williamstown in 1996, *La Ronde* at Williamstown in 1997, *Waiting for Lefty* at the Blue Light Theatre Company in 1997, *The Big Knife* at Williamstown in 1998, *The Constant Wife* at the Westport Playhouse in 2000, and *Three Days of Rain* at the Westport Playhouse in 2001.

Joanne Woodward's first two leading film roles were in *Count Three and Pray* in 1955 and *A Kiss Before Dying* in 1956. Woodward continued to star in feature films over the next forty years, including *The Three Faces of Eve* (1957), *No Down Payment* (1957), *The Long, Hot Summer* (1958), *Rally Round the Flag, Boys!* (1958), *The Sound and the Fury* (1959), *The Fugitive Kind* (1960), *From the Terrace* (1960), *Paris Blues* (1961), *The Stripper* (1963), *A New Kind of Love* (1963), *Signpost to Murder* (1964), *A Big Hand for the Little Lady* (1966), *A Fine Madness* (1966), *Rachel, Rachel* (1968), *Winning* (1969), *WUSA* (1970), *They Might Be Giants* (1971), *The Effect of Gamma Rays on Man-in-the-Moon Marigolds* (1972), *Summer Wishes, Winter Dreams* (1973), *The Drowning Pool* (1975), *The End* (1978), *Harry & Son* (1984), *The Glass Menagerie* (1987), *Mr. & Mrs. Bridge* (1990), *Philadelphia* (1993), and *The Age of Innocence* (1993).

Woodward also starred in made-for-television dramas, including *All the Way Home* (1971), *Sybil* (1976), *Little Women* (1976), *Come Back, Little Sheba* (1977), *See How She Runs* (1978), *A Christmas to Remember* (1978), *The Streets of LA* (1979), *The Shadow Box* (1980), *Crisis at Central High* (1981), *Passions* (1984), *Do You Remember Love* (1985), *Foreign Affairs* (1993), *Blind Spot* (1993), *Breathing Lessons* (1994), and *Empire Falls* (2005). She has narrated several feature-length historical documentaries and performed voice-over character roles in selected dramatic productions for film and television. Woodward directed *Thanksgiving* for Icarus and Spelling-Goldberg/ABC in 1979, and the original screen adaptation of *Come Along with Me* for American Playhouse/PBS in 1982. Her producing and co-producing credits include *Broadway's Dreamers: The Legacy of the Group Theatre* for American Masters/PBS in 1989, *Blind Spot* for CBS in 1993, *Our Town* for Showtime in 2003, and *Lucky Them* for IFC Films in 2013.

Joanne Woodward's awards include National Board of Review Award for Best Actress in 1957 for *The Three Faces of Eve* and *No Down Payment*, Academy Award for Best Actress and Golden Globe Award for Best Actress in a Motion Picture Drama in 1958 for *The Three Faces of Eve*, Hasty Pudding Theatricals Woman of the Year in 1959, San Sebastián International Film Festival Zulueta Prize for Best Actress in 1960 for *The Fugitive Kind*, New York Film Critics Circle Award for Best Actress and Kansas City Film Critics Circle Award for Best Actress in 1968 for *Rachel, Rachel*, Golden Globe Award for Best Actress in a Motion Picture Drama in 1969 for *Rachel, Rachel*, Cannes Film Festival Award for Best Actress and Kansas City Film Critics Circle Award for Best Actress in 1973 for *The Effect of Gamma Rays on Man-in-the-Moon Marigolds*, New York Film Critics Circle Award for Best Actress and Kansas City Film Critics Circle Award for Best Actress in 1974 for *Summer Wishes, Winter Dreams*, BAFTA Film Award for Best Actress in 1975 for *Summer Wishes, Winter Dreams*, Film Society of Lincoln Center Gala Tribute in 1975 (with Paul Newman), Primetime Emmy Award for Outstanding Lead Actress in a Drama or Comedy Special in 1978 for *See How She Runs*, Primetime Emmy Award for Outstanding Lead Actress in a Drama or Comedy Special in 1985 for *Do You Remember Love*, Screen Actors Guild Life Achievement Award in 1985 (with Paul Newman), Primetime Emmy Award for Outstanding Informational Special in 1990 for *Broadway's Dreamers: The Legacy of the Group Theatre*, New York Film Critics Circle Award for Best Actress and Kansas City Film Critics Circle Award for Best Actress in 1990 for *Mr. & Mrs. Bridge*, Roosevelt Institute Four Freedoms Award in 1991 (with Paul Newman), Kennedy Center Honors in the Performing Arts in 1992 (with Paul Newman), Jefferson Award for Public Service in 1994 (with Paul Newman), and Golden Globe Award for Best Performance by an Actress in a Miniseries or Motion Picture Made for Television and Screen Actors Guild Award for Outstanding Performance by a Female Actor in a TV Movie or Miniseries in 1995 for *Breathing Lessons*.

Woodward was Artistic Director of the Westport Country Playhouse from 2001 through 2005. Under her stewardship, a thirty-million-dollar capital campaign was undertaken, modernizing the Playhouse's existing facility and surrounding campus, sustaining its transition from summer stock to year-round theatre, expanding internship, educational, and community engagement programs, and strengthening its endowment. Woodward also attracted to Westport a roster of significant productions with prominent actors and directors, and sponsored the development and production of new theatrical works, considerably elevating the theatre's profile.

Woodward is a major supporter of the performing arts and an advocate for human rights, nuclear disarmament, environmental conservation, and medical research. She chaired the National Women's Conference to Prevent Nuclear War and has served on the boards of the Environmental Defense Fund, the Center for Defense Information, New York City Center, and Sarah Lawrence College. With her daughter Nell, she funds the Nell Newman Foundation, awarding grants to individuals and organizations dedicated to the environment, education, arts and culture, scientific research, emergency relief, and international relations.

Joanne Woodward married Paul Newman in 1958. In addition to stepchildren Scott, Susan, and Stephanie, they had three daughters, Nell, Melissa, and Clea, and two grandchildren, Peter and Henry. She is retired from public life and lives in Westport, Connecticut.

With Nell, New York, 1959 (Paul Newman)

With Nell and Melissa, Westport, Connecticut, 1963 (Joanne Woodward)

With Susan, Stephanie, Nell, and Melissa, Beverly Hills, 1967

Paul Newman

(1925–2008)

Paul Newman was an American actor, director, producer, philanthropist, political activist, and championship racecar driver. He was born in Cleveland, Ohio, in 1925 and was raised in Shaker Heights. Following his service in the United States Navy during World War II in the Pacific Theatre, Newman attended Kenyon College, graduating with a Bachelor of Arts degree in drama and economics in 1949.

He married his first wife, Jackie Witte, in 1949, while they were members of the Belfry Players, a summer stock theatre in Delavan, Wisconsin. The following year, they joined the Woodstock Players in Woodstock, Illinois, soon thereafter moving to New Haven, Connecticut, where Newman enrolled in the master's program at Yale University's Department of Drama, School of Fine Arts, in the fall of 1951. In 1952, he moved to New York City and began studying at The Actors Studio under Lee Strasberg. During this time, Newman appeared in numerous early live television dramatic anthology series, including *Tales of Tomorrow* (1952), *Suspense* (1952), *The Aldrich Family* (1952–53), *The Web* (1952–53), *You Are There* (1953), *The Man Behind the Badge* (1953–54), *Goodyear Playhouse* (1954), *Armstrong Circle Theatre* (1954), *The United States Steel Hour* (1954–56), *Appointment with Adventure* (1955), *The Philco Television Playhouse* (1955), *Producer's Showcase* (1955), *Playwrights '56* (1955), *The Kaiser Aluminum Hour* (1956), and *Playhouse 90* (1958). In 1953, Newman made his Broadway debut in the original production of William Inge's *Picnic* at the Music Box Theatre, and in 1955 he played the lead in *The Desperate Hours* by Joseph Hayes at the Ethel Barrymore Theatre. His other Broadway and regional stage credits include *Sweet Bird of Youth* at the Martin Beck Theatre in 1959–60, *Baby Want a Kiss* at the Little Theatre in 1964, *Ancestral Voices* at the Westport Country Playhouse in 2000, *Our Town* at the Westport Playhouse and the Booth Theatre in 2002, and *Trumbo* at the Ridgefield Playhouse in 2004.

Paul Newman made his film debut in *The Silver Chalice* in 1954, followed by his first successful leading role as Rocky Graziano in *Somebody Up There Likes Me* in 1956. Newman starred in feature films over the next forty years, including *The Rack* (1956), *Until They Sail* (1957), *The Helen Morgan Story* (1957), *The Long, Hot Summer* (1957), *Cat on a Hot Tin Roof* (1958), *The Left Handed Gun* (1958), *Rally Round the Flag, Boys!* (1958), *The Young Philadelphians* (1959), *From the Terrace* (1960), *Exodus* (1960), *The Hustler* (1961), *Paris Blues* (1961), *Sweet Bird of Youth* (1962), *Hemingway's Adventures of a Young Man* (1962), *Hud* (1963), *A New Kind of Love* (1963), *The Prize* (1963), *What a Way to Go!* (1964), *The Outrage* (1964), *Lady L* (1965), *Harper* (1966), *Torn Curtain* (1966), *Hombre* (1967), *Cool Hand Luke* (1967), *The Secret War of Harry Frigg* (1968), *Winning* (1969), *Butch Cassidy and the Sundance Kid* (1969), *WUSA* (1970), *Sometimes a Great Notion* (1970), *The Life and Times of Judge Roy Bean* (1972), *Pocket Money* (1972), *The Mackintosh Man* (1973), *The Sting* (1973), *The*

Towering Inferno (1974), *The Drowning Pool* (1975), *Buffalo Bill and the Indians, or Sitting Bull's History Lesson* (1976), *Slap Shot* (1977), *Quintet* (1979), *When Time Ran Out* (1980), *Fort Apache, The Bronx* (1981), *Absence of Malice* (1981), *The Verdict* (1982), *Harry & Son* (1984), *The Color of Money* (1986), *Fat Man and Little Boy* (1989), *Blaze* (1989), *Mr. & Mrs. Bridge* (1990), *The Hudsucker Proxy* (1994), *Nobody's Fool* (1994), *Twilight* (1998), *Message in a Bottle* (1999), *Where the Money Is* (2000), and *Road to Perdition* (2002). Newman also hosted and narrated *Once Upon a Wheel* for ABC Television in 1971, and starred in *Our Town* for Showtime in 2003 and *Empire Falls* for HBO in 2005. Newman was producer or co-producer of ten of the above titles, and for *They Might Be Giants* (1971).

As a director, Newman's credits include *Rachel, Rachel* (1968), *Sometimes a Great Notion* (1970), *The Effect of Gamma Rays on Man-in-the-Moon Marigolds* (1972), *The Shadow Box* (1980), *Harry & Son* (1984), and *The Glass Menagerie* (1987).

Paul Newman's awards include Golden Globe Award for Most Promising Newcomer for *The Silver Chalice* in 1957, Cannes Film Festival Award for Best Actor in 1958 for *The Long, Hot Summer*, BAFTA Film Award for Best Foreign Actor in a Leading Role in 1962 for *The Hustler*, Cinema Writers Circle Award for Best Foreign Actor in 1962 for *Somebody Up There Likes Me*, New York Film Critics Circle Award for Best Director in 1968 for *Rachel, Rachel*, Hasty Pudding Theatricals Man of the Year in 1968, Golden Globe Award for Best Director in 1969 for *Rachel, Rachel*, Film Society of Lincoln Center Gala Tribute in 1975 (with Joanne Woodward), David di Donatello Award for Best Foreign Actor in 1983 for *The Verdict*, Golden Globe Cecil B. DeMille Award in 1984, Honorary Award given by the Academy of Motion Picture Arts and Sciences presented in 1986, Screen Actors Guild Life Achievement Award in 1985 (with Joanne Woodward), National Board of Review Award for Best Actor in 1986 for *The Color of Money*, Academy Award for Best Actor in 1987 for *The Color of Money*, Roosevelt Institute Four Freedoms Award in 1991 (with Joanne Woodward), Kennedy Center Honors in the Performing Arts in 1992 (with Joanne Woodward), Jean Hersholt Humanitarian Award given by the Academy of Motion Picture Arts and Sciences in 1994, Jefferson Award for Public Service in 1994 (with Joanne Woodward), New York Film Critics Circle Award for Best Actor in 1994 for *Nobody's Fool*, Berlin International Film Festival Silver Bear Award for Best Actor and National Society of Film Critics Award for Best Actor in 1995 for *Nobody's Fool*, Primetime Emmy Award for Outstanding Supporting Actor in a Miniseries or a Movie in 2005 for *Empire Falls*, and Golden Globe Award for Best Performance by an Actor in a Supporting Role in a Series, Miniseries or Motion Picture Made for Television and Screen Actors Guild Award for Outstanding Performance by a Male Actor in a Miniseries or Television Movie in 2006 for *Empire Falls*.

Newman's Own food company was established by Paul Newman in 1982, and during his lifetime distributed all after-tax profits to a broad range of charitable causes. In 1988, Newman founded The Hole in the Wall Gang Camp in Ashford, Connecticut, offering year-round programs onsite, in hospitals, clinics, and campers' homes and their communities, serving more than twenty thousand children and their family members annually. He also founded the SeriousFun Children's Network, a global community of campsites and programs for children with cancer and other serious medical conditions. Newman founded The Committee to Encourage Corporate Philanthropy in 1999, Newman's Own Foundation in 2005, and Safe Water Network in 2006.

Newman was a prominent political activist, lending his personal endorsement and financial support to candidates for state and national office, and to organized social movements devoted to issues of racial equity, nuclear disarmament, environmental justice, global warming, and the hazards of corporate monopoly. In 1994, Newman partnered with Victor Navasky and E. L. Doctorow to purchase and endow *The Nation*, the oldest continuously published magazine in the United States. Through the years, he sponsored a series of fundraising events for the publication and was an attending contributor to its editorial pages. Newman was also president of The Actors Studio from 1983 to 1995.

Paul Newman began car racing while training for his performance in the 1969 film *Winning* at the Bob Bondurant School of High Performance Driving at Orange County International Raceway. Coming to the sport relatively late in life, Newman was formally introduced to competitive driving by Sam Posey and Bob Sharp in Formula Vees at Lime Rock Park in Lakeville, Connecticut, in 1971, and a year later joined Bob Sharp Racing, driving the Datsun 510B sedan in the SCCA Northeast Division. In 1976, he founded Newman Freeman Racing Team with Bill Freeman, competing in Can-Am, IndyCar, and other high-performance vehicles in multiple SCCA- and IMSA-sponsored events. He was awarded the SCCA President's Cup the same year. In 1979, Newman finished second overall and first in class in the 24 Hours of Le Mans with Dick Barbour and Rolf Stommelen. Newman won four first-place SCCA National Championships, in 1976, 1979, 1985, and 1986, a Trans-Am race at Brainerd International Raceway in 1982, and a Trans-Am race at Lime Rock Park in 1986, and finished third overall and first in class in the Rolex 24 Hours of Daytona in 1995 for Roush Racing. He founded Newman/Haas Racing with Carl Haas in 1983. Newman/Haas competed in the CART and IndyCar Series through 2011, winning over a hundred CART/Champ Car races and eight season championships. In 2006, he formed the Champ Car Atlantic team Newman Wachs Racing with Eddie Wachs. Newman completed his final championship race at Lime Rock in 2007, driving a 700-horsepower Corvette carrying the number 82, his age at the time. He was posthumously inducted into the SCCA Hall of Fame in 2009.

Paul Newman had three children, Scott, Susan, and Stephanie, with his first wife. He married Joanne Woodward in 1958, and they had three daughters, Nell, Melissa, and Clea, and two grandsons, Peter and Henry. He died in 2008 in Westport, Connecticut, at the age of 83.

Joanne Woodward & Paul Newman

HEAD OVER HEELS

A Love Affair in Words and Pictures

Voracious / Little, Brown and Company
Hachette Book Group
1290 Avenue of the Americas, New York, NY 10104
voraciousbooks.com

First Edition: October 2023

Voracious is an imprint of Little, Brown and Company, a division of Hachette Book Group, Inc.
The Voracious name and logo are trademarks of Hachette Book Group, Inc.

The publisher is not responsible for websites (or their content) that are not owned by the publisher.

The Hachette Speakers Bureau provides a wide range of authors for speaking events. To find out more, go to hachettespeakersbureau.com or email hachettespeakers@hbgusa.com.

Little, Brown and Company books may be purchased in bulk for business, educational, or promotional use. For information, please contact your local bookseller or the Hachette Book Group Special Markets Department at special.markets@hbgusa.com.

Except where otherwise noted, all photographs provided by the author.

Edited by Andrew Kelly

Designed by Dan Miller Design, New York

Endpapers: Beverly Hills, 1963 (David Sutton)

ISBN 9780316526005
LCCN 2022952077

10 9 8 7 6 5 4 3 2 1

IM

Printed in China